Greig is self-employed, working with the adventure tourism industry and also as a leadership training and personal development facilitator. He has written for hunting and wildlife magazines and his first book was published in 2009.

He lives in Nelson and at 55 years 'young' is still keen to be out amongst wild horizons with pack and rifle.

WILD HORIZONS

MORE GREAT HUNTING ADVENTURES

GREIG CAIGOU

HarperCollins*Publishers*

This book is dedicated to
Gordon and Natalie Max.

And written as a legacy for future
generations of New Zealand hunters.

HarperCollins*Publishers*

First published in 2011
by HarperCollins*Publishers* (New Zealand) Limited
PO Box 1, Shortland Street, Auckland 1140

Copyright © Greig Caigou 2011

Greig Caigou asserts the moral right to be identified as the author of this work.
All rights reserved. No part of this publication may be reproduced, stored in
a retrieval system or transmitted in any form or by any means, electronic,
mechanical, photocopying, recording or otherwise, without the prior written
permission of the publishers.

HarperCollins*Publishers*
31 View Road, Glenfield, Auckland 0627, New Zealand
Level 13, 201 Elizabeth Street, Sydney NSW 2000, Australia
A 53, Sector 57, Noida, UP, India
77–85 Fulham Palace Road, London W6 8JB, United Kingdom
2 Bloor Street East, 20th floor, Toronto, Ontario M4W 1A8, Canada
10 East 53rd Street, New York, NY 10022, USA

National Library of New Zealand Cataloguing-in-Publication Data

Caigou, Greig.
Wild horizons : more great hunting adventures / Greig Caigou.
ISBN 978-1-86950-878-4
1. Big game hunting—New Zealand.
I Title.
799.26092—dc 22

ISBN: 978 1 86950 878 4

Cover design by Xou Creative
Front cover image by Greig Caigou; back cover image by Matt Winter (www.
wildnaturenewzealand.co.nz)
Typesetting by Springfield West

Printed by Griffin Press, Australia

70gsm Classic used by HarperCollins*Publishers* is a natural, recyclable product
made from wood grown in sustainable forests. The manufacturing processes
conform to the environmental regulations in the country of origin, Finland.

Contents

Preface

When I wrote my first-ever hunting book I had wanted to catch the essence of what hunting was about for me.

The attraction is the sense of adventure — getting out into the back-country and stepping up to the challenges we face from the environment, our quarry and sometimes from ourselves. The reliance on self and some hardihood adds to the overall rewards, and that *Hunting Adventures* book was a step into some of the stories I'd lived and some of my reflections while out there making memories.

Feedback from readers was very good and the aspect most enjoyed was that they were not just hunting stories but that there was also a thoughtful theme running through the book.

This book has the same theme!

If adventuring was what drew me out hunting, I wondered if this was true for other hunters. The more people I spoke with, the more this rang true.

Here, in this book, I've tried to get inside the most memorable hunting adventures of five other hunters from throughout the eras of hunting in New Zealand. The range covers a now very elderly Gordon Max, who grew up in the company of some of the grand old masters of hunting. There is some storytelling from Zeff Veronese who immigrated to New Zealand especially in search of an outdoors El Dorado. He still hunts — and gets out more than most — despite his 70-plus years.

And then I've captured memorable hunts from some younger hunters. There's a 'Generation X' hunter, Jansen Travis, who was introduced to hunting by his still mad-keen father and there's also 17-year-old Jessica McLees representing a young woman, new to hunting and sharing her best time out after big game in the hills around Monowai in Western Southland. I've added in another young hunter, Simon Buschl, from my local area in Nelson. These folk are representative New Zealanders.

But what makes hunting special for these people?

My goal is to reveal the special and memorable elements of their classic hunts and discover the common threads, as well as what it is that we must retain in our hunting heritage for the next generations. Along the way I also share some more stories of my own, not only about memorable hunting moments but also about special places to go hunting. Again, it is these regions and the opportunities they offer that contribute to classic hunting adventures for me.

As I spend time in the hunter's Holy Grail of Fiordland, the intimidating South Westland interior and the magic snowgrass tops of Canterbury or Nelson, I want you to read how my passion for hunting is so strongly linked to my enthusiasm for these wild places and therefore for wilderness preservation.

This is a book of hunting stories. This is about authentic, 'fair-chase' hunting in New Zealand: what makes it special, what we absolutely *must* preserve and promote as worthy of retaining, and the kinds of individual responsibilities we each have for this legacy and with our own hunter's creed.

Acknowledgments

I have thoroughly enjoyed revisiting my own hunts and reliving them through the telling of these stories. So I am thankful for my lovely wife, Marijke, and her support and long-suffering each time I've headed for the 'writer's couch'. You don't write books about hunting in New Zealand to make money; rather you write them because you're interested in doing so and to leave a legacy for other generations of hunters. In this and other respects, Marijke has backed me. Thanks, honey.

I have also been richly treated in this project from the relationships formed with the other hunters whose stories are told here. To Gordon Max, Zeff Veronese, Jansen Travis, Simon Buschl and Jessica McLees — thank you for your time and the opportunities to share so many other stories as well.

I'd especially like to thank Zeff for the candid insights into your life story and the enthusiasm you still have for the hunting life. This is infectious for me still, as it was all those years ago when I met you for the first time as a youngster in the New Zealand Deerstalkers Association (NZDA).

The hours spent with Gordon and Natalie Max have been such a blessing, too, that I've dedicated this book to them, hoping that the respect I have for them both is portrayed as part of the legacy of this book. Gordon is a gentleman of the 'old school' with values I admire and with a deep and full respect for the animal kingdom, wild places and the life of a hunter. Thank you, Gordon, for providing an example that I hope I can emulate.

In this book I have again been ably assisted by Grant Irvine as he's read and reread chapters to pick up on spelling or grammatical errors and to suggest ways to better craft my word flow. Thanks, mate.

Howard Egan was called up from my past connections with the NZDA and very kindly gave some overview to these chapters. I may not have reached the high literary standards he set or taken all his suggestions on board but his big-picture perspective has certainly been invaluable. So, too, has Aaron Meikle, who has been crucial in the development of my philosophy. He has introduced me to some great thinkers in the hunting world and continues to enlarge my horizons by providing links to worthy resources. A challenging thinker — I am indebted to you in this respect.

A range of photographers supported this project. They are all the travelling companions of the hunters involved, who have taken up the camera to record the moments. They include my daughter Emma and those who are credited alongside their images. Matt Winter provided me a few superb shots of game animals in the wild. Check out his website at www. wildnaturenewzealand.co.nz to more fully appreciate his excellent stalking and camera skills in the field.

Finally, a big thanks to the team at HarperCollins who have stepped up to support a novice author. In time, maybe we can do it again, but first I'll need to go do some more research … out hunting!

Chapter 1

Fiordland draws us in

Perhaps it was fitting I had no camera at the ready. As a result, the brief scene had to be more vividly burned into my memory as a classic hunting moment.

On a steep angle above me, there was Murray climbing purposefully towards the rugged skyline with a heavy rack of antlers protruding wide from his pack as he slogged upwards into the void! What a great sight. It summed up so much of that trip for me. With chest pumping from the exertion of the climb, I swung about so my gaze took in everything else: great vistas of wilderness, mist-shrouded hills, with patches of expansive tussock basins below and mountains everywhere — far and wide.

Absolutely fantastic.

It's enormous country, where images and memories like these are fully earned!

Fiordland is everything it promises.

And for this trip, Fiordland had delivered on everything I'd wanted — and needed!

Fiordland represents the Holy Grail of New Zealand hunting, and with that in mind my friend Murray Elwood and I had ventured there again in 2010. For some time we'd been thinking of trying a trip in February to take advantage of the more settled weather and wapiti bulls being out on the tops, putting on condition before the mating season. When the opportunity presented itself to be able to squeeze out 10 days in February, away from our responsibilities at home, we quickly decided to head for the hills and set about putting a plan together.

We knew the bulls would be in hard antler so the main objective was to get back into the headwaters of the Lugar Burn where we'd spied a big wapiti bull several years earlier. We did value the route-finding knowledge we'd built up on a previous trip, but we also wanted to look over new country, so I'd sat looking at the map pondering other routes into the headwaters. I remembered sitting on the ridge at the head of the McDougall branch of the Lugar Burn and liked the look and ease of travel along the tops over towards the head of the Henderson Burn. That looked pretty enticing on the map, too, so the plan quickly hatched for a trip up the Glaisnock River and into the Henderson Burn to its headwaters. From there we could access the ridges all around and be well positioned to come in on the head basins of the Lugar Burn, Wapiti River and Canyon Creek as well as allow for easy forays towards the Edith Saddle country.

Moir's Guide detailed the route into the Henderson in fairly nonchalant terms and the gradients upriver looked easy and so appealing! Surely, there wouldn't be any nasty travel as we'd struck above the forks in the Lugar Burn gorge. (However, a few weeks later, pushing through a monster rock garden after six hours of slog, we sure felt out of touch again with Fiordland travel and 'easy' routes!)

So the planning got under way and great Southern hospitality was again sorted by my friend Chris Howden, who arranged for a local farmer to drop us into North Fiord of Lake Te Anau in his boat. Tentage and food buying was next to be organized and Murray and I quickly determined that we'd take a small tent and a fly, allowing us some variations in how we could move about the country, especially since we both use bivvy bags. We knew as well that we had no time to build up any extra fitness prior to the trip so the weight of gear was a factor we had to be ruthless in guarding.

Now there is not much weight that can be saved with standard kit; however, most hunters I meet take far too many clothes, ammunition, other 'extras' and gadgets. We kept our standard outdoor and hunting gear light and clothing layers to a minimum. It's surprising how little gear you actually ever really need. This time I was also carrying a locator beacon for us both. For me, the real weight was going to come in the form of two cameras, one still and one video, so some better effort was made in trying to get food weight down while maximizing energy per gram. Once all gear was divided up, my pack came in easily under 20 kilos before the cameras went in.

Murray did laugh, however, when he noticed me still undecided whether to take just the five rounds of ammo I'd allowed or to throw in the spare three extras I had in my gun bag! My rationale has always been it takes only one shot to down an animal but a couple extra are useful as backup. I wasn't going to be shooting lots of animals so just a few rounds were needed. Many hunters carry way more than this for a contingency such as banging their scope out of alignment, but with two rifles between us this possibility was covered anyway.

Food was largely the two-person dehydrated meals to which we'd add extra water and supplement with extra rice or spud flakes. (Couscous, dehydrated spuds or veges and instant gravy sachets are light, quick and really rate for energy value, too.) I also carry protein powder for extra drinks to aid recovery after big days and we use dehy onions or soup mixes to supplement meals of fried heart or liver from any animals we shoot. Tea, Milo and oats round out the menu along with One Square Meal bars. Importantly, these meals require minimal preparation time, which therefore requires less fuel for cookers and sure helps when having dinner quite late after a long day on the hill.

The time grew close very quickly and most hunters will relate well to that final desperate cramming of home jobs that need to be sorted before you can leave family and get on the road. Somehow, despite several days of preparation time, Murray and I still found ourselves trying to get odd jobs done at close to midnight when we'd also agreed to meet up at 3.30 a.m. for the long drive south!

With a late change of plans we'd decided to take Murray's tin boat and pull this behind the ute all the way to Te Anau. That way, we could have the flexibility to come out earlier or move locations, as opposed to being stuck at the Glaisnock awaiting a boat for pick-up.

The trip south was a long one and the early departure was part of a grand plan to travel down the West Coast and get to

Te Anau in time to cross the lake in the calm of evening. Then we'd walk up the Glaisnock to the junction of the Henderson Burn to break the swagging part of the overall trip. Suffice to say, we made it to Harihari before an enforced delay of three hours due to a collapsed wheel bearing on the trailer. Some rescue work had the local mechanic drilling a new stud pattern into an old hub found 'out back' and we got under way in time to pep up our journey with coffee at Fox Glacier township. In Queenstown we devoured a monster 'Ferg burger' and this was the only other stop on a relentless driving mission.

Even with the long southern twilight, we arrived at Lake Te Anau virtually on dark and so gave away any thought of a night crossing, especially when greeted with a howling wind throwing up great waves on the lake. We'd had enough of the 14 hours on our bum by then so we pushed along towards Te Anau Downs, keeping one bleary eye out for a lay-by in which we could collapse into our sleeping bags. Soon enough we came upon a cutting off to our left and did a U-turn to bring us back to what turned out to be a popular little nook for backpacker tourist vans. These folk were all safely shacked away in their colourful Escape rental vans when we made an entrance and stretched further down the narrow track towards the lakeshore. By this time it was spitting from the blustery northwest and neither of us fancied getting out the tent and starting the next day with wet gear. We weren't fussed about cramming into the cab of the ute either! But necessity is the mother of invention, and so I informed Murray that we didn't need a tent when we had a tin one on the trailer!

With that revelation we soon had the tinnie off the trailer, flipped over upside down and leaned on the rear of the trailer, making a nice cover from the elements. The French backpacker couple in their clapped-out VW Kombi who came late, looking hopefully for some space, must have wondered about our low-spec motor holiday and the make-do approach of Kiwis. Before long we crawled underneath and were going to sleep with the melodious sound of rain on a tin roof.

Te Anau Downs was still and eerie the next morning, and with final checks completed we pushed off with the little 15 horse idling us out into the bay.

At the gateway to Fiordland wapiti hunts — Te Anau Downs. *Greig Caigou*

What a fantastic sense of mission comes over you when the adventure is about to begin! Sure it had been a bit of an epic drive, especially after cramming in all the home jobs first, and sure there had been a level of excitement as we slept under the tin boat the evening before, but now we were finally on the way. We soaked in the moment ... its energy, excitement and the expectation of what lay ahead. Fiordland was about to dish it all up for us.

Wilderness draws us in — heading into the North Arm of Lake Te Anau. *Greig Caigou*

Murray gunned the little motor to full noise as we turned out into the lake proper. We slipped across the inky glass of water as daylight glowed to full strength out to the east. It was going to be a cracker day, and part of what I love about the boat ride is the way Fiordland starts to gather in around you as you zip along with the crisp air on your face. At first it's the expanse of the lake, but soon enough you're whisking past forest-fringed bays and steep shoreline before rounding into North Fiord and feeling those great rock ramparts towering above you. Looming up ahead is the bigger stuff of mountains and adventure. A feeling of the wild envelops you and closes out all sense of civilization or other people, and the awareness of your smallness amid these natural things is all so powerful. This is the 'nearby faraway' that American hunting author David Petersen mentions, a magnificent place just out in the backyard of Te Anau and only 12 hours' drive from Nelson. It is the wilderness of Fiordland.

Soon enough the Narrows is before us and we glide through with dark, sunken 'tree monsters' beneath. Here precipitous peaks preside over the murky depths and we soak in the panoramas of clearing blue sky that beckons from beyond the bush-clad lakeshore ahead. Murray can feel the current of the Glaisnock as we cut the revs and glide towards shore.

Surprisingly, there is only one other boat here, a small inflatable, pulled up on the fine gravel. Before long we have the tinnie well up on the bank with a chain connecting it and the outboard to a tree. The resident mongrel sandflies keep a sense of urgency to our tasks even though I was prepared by wearing overtrousers. Before long we're hoisting our burdens and making a short foray up to Glaisnock Hut.

Intentions are written in the hut book and we both check out just what else has been happening by way of parties coming into the area. Most seem to be fishermen, of those that have bothered to add any information, and so without much ado we strike out in the direction of the track marker beside the hut.

We have a few comments to make about the absence of a

big clear track, despite the marker, but this is fully in line with a conservation policy that retains a sense of wilderness by restricting access or making access difficult. No immediate track means that only those prepared for what lies beyond will be entering there … and this is good. Sadly, this has recently changed, with blue markers up to the log crossing.

Soon enough, of course, you end up alongside the Glaisnock River and there is a fully developed deer trail along the banks. As this is such an access valley to the rest of the mountains and valleys beyond, the travelling is easy, and within an hour and a half we are at the Henderson Burn grabbing a drink before turning up-valley on the true right bank as per *Moir's Guide*.

The deer trail gains height very quickly here and strikes a narrow spur with a great view of the constricted chasm and waterfall. It's a beauty and with a sense of the going being easy we continue up the trail, climbing higher and higher and increasingly away from the noise of the river. Still the pathway seems quite evident and I'm adamant that if you find such a strong deer trail in Fiordland you stick to it like glue, as the animals know what they are doing. However, after a time the trail seemed to be leading back along the Glaisnock itself and we resolve to strike out back around into the Henderson Burn proper, thinking that surely we'd gained sufficient height to sidle around above the bottom gorge. This is the way of bush travel, we thought: you gain height to get around gorges and then you gradually descend to the easy going in the valley floor!

The going at that altitude proved just plain annoying, and we worked up and down trying to find a good level between windfall trees and thickly vegetated gullies. The mind game had started again, and I found my fortitude slipping with every exertion over and through each new obstacle in what was turning out to be a continuous clutter of undergrowth barring our progress. The toil and heat of the day worked the sweat out of us and we knew we were making hard work of it. An hour turned into two and at that stage we were truly frustrated. I could make out a high point through the trees across on the other side of the valley so while I sat down to correlate my watch altimeter with a compass bearing on that high point, Murray fired up his GPS.

What a revelation that turned out to be! We'd come all of 1.5 kilometres in two hours and there was no way *Moir's* travelling time of six to eight hours to gain the head of the valley was going to work at that rate of progress. Obviously, I had lived too long between trips into this country. Coming from the top of the South Island we were used to much more open travel in beech forest, so this pace of travel was frustrating and annoyingly slow. (You need to redefine your expectations when in this country and you certainly don't cover the amount of territory you think you can when poring over maps in the comfort of home.)

The saying 'If you keep doing what you've always done, you'll keep getting what you've always got' came to mind, and so there was nothing for it but to try a different tactic if we wanted to make better progress.

Now alpine hunters, like myself, don't like to give away altitude, but it was plainly obvious that we needed to drop to the river and try the going down there, especially as the route guide had said the trail followed the true right bank. We'd obviously gone too high, missing any turn-off once past the chasm, and were instead sidling through gut after gut of slow going.

We angled down, and once we made the river's edge immediately struck some good deer trails. With a lift to the spirits, we put in some fast sections, gaining altitude at about 100 metres an hour through the middle sections of the Henderson Burn.

In time the river started to narrow and there was a sense of foreboding that the relatively good passage was coming to an end. Soon enough, we entered an otherworldly domain of thick moss, vines and monster rocks right down to the river's edge. We struggled on through these, criss-crossing the stream to check if there was better travelling on the other side, and then at other times following faint deer leads that would track further into the rock garden. But before long these would fade, only to reveal instead a labyrinth of hidden drops that threatened to break a tired leg should we lose attention. Obviously, in some olden era great masses of the local canyon had sheared off the mountainside, tumbling down to the river below, finally settling in a confused jumble of rock in which we now battled onwards at a slower rate again.

But then that's Fiordland. That was why I was there, wasn't it? For the challenges of testing my resilience and digging deeper for that mental, physical and emotional capacity. At times it all just seemed too hard and a breather or snack-stop would be called to provide a physical freshen-up and also to allow some talk or banter to lessen the mental load we were each carrying. Then it would be back to duelling with the mind, the body and the undergrowth!

Struggling along at one time I recalled the old Indian yarn of a chief sitting with his braves around a fire and telling a story of two wolves that fight each other all the days of our life. One wolf stands for courage and tells you that things are possible. This 'good wolf' represents positive thinking and energy. The 'bad wolf' wants you to put things off and says things cannot be done and wears your resolve down. One of the young braves asked the chief, 'But, great chief, which wolf wins this battle in life?' The chief wisely replied, 'The one you feed the most!'

I knew, at times, I was battling with the 'bad wolf', allowing myself to get frustrated with the slow progress, sore shoulders, the sweat and dirt and grovelling under logs that were just lower than I needed them to be. I knew that instead I should be feeding the good wolf. Some positive 'self-talk' was needed and I had to focus on the progress we were making. After all, there was no real timetable! I had to remember that this wasn't a marked track but was rather a touch closer to the more genuine and natural connection to wilderness that I craved. I had to focus on how I knew I'd be able to look back on this tougher part and more fully appreciate the views and other things later on. I had to concentrate on helping Murray with his battling, too, and how we could motivate each other through the hard slog.

(It seems to me that many stories of hunts in Fiordland tell little of the actual drama of getting into the hunting grounds and even downplay them to some extent, so I think it's worth sharing some of these toils which set the scene for many of my classic hunting moments, and in fact are a key ingredient of them.)

By refocusing what I gave thought to, I steadily picked up energy for the mission at hand, and in time we started to capture glimpses of open tops ahead and the object of our efforts.

At one stage I led down into the streambed and caught a movement behind some scrub on the opposite bank. On a small clearing a wapiti cow was feeding, ears twitching as she chewed, unaware of our presence. We were able to get some good close-up footage of her feeding with occasional rays of afternoon light on her sleek flanks. Shortly, she was joined by her young one and we watched from only 20 metres for some time before walking straight towards her to see her reaction. With fawn close behind she moved off 50 metres towards some ribbonwood, stopping and checking us again before ambling off into the thicket.

With that distraction and with increasing open areas in the bush, our spirits had lifted and after eight hours' travel since leaving the lake we could see the headwater flats just ahead. While angling through the last of the forest I noticed a very large, house-sized rock out on its own in the flat of the bush and with a keen eye out for a possible camp site I deviated to check it out. What a find that turned out to be, for here, just 100 metres from the bush edge, was a perfect spot under the lee of this great rock. The rock sits on the true left of the river and on the downstream side offers fully upright headroom and dry accommodation for several people. (Other parties had used the rock in the past and if I had done more research prior to our trip I would have learned of this in advance. Still, it's more fun discovering these things for yourself at times.)

We dropped our packs with a great sense of relief.

Even though we were still tired we couldn't help ourselves from grabbing binos, rifles and camera and heading the last remaining paces through the bush to check out the head basin. We knew the breeze was in our favour and this is so important in these valleys. As we moved to a glassing position, we watched a cow and a yearling close by on the terrace across the river.

Our rock shelter. *Greig Caigou*

The head of the Henderson Burn is a lovely combination of open flats with a slow stream meandering through them and with ribbonwood, thick crown fern and scrub fingers extending down into the flats. There are the usual steep slopes on either side with all manner of plausible access points to the upper

FIORDLAND DRAWS US IN

slopes and the headwall has a waterfall, above which you can easily imagine a further large hanging basin. Tucked in beside some crown fern with good rests, it wasn't long before deer were spotted in the headwall, and the first one Murray picked up had antlers. Woo-hoo!

Some indecision entered the ranks now because Murray was feeling pretty done in from our swagging, and seeing it was so late anyway he wanted to leave the animals there until morning. I agreed that perhaps he was right, but I threw in a seed of doubt in pointing out that anything can happen overnight, such as a wind or weather change and the circumstances might be different next morning. After all, a 'bull in hand is worth two in the bush'! I felt we could get across the open ground to within range quite quickly, too, despite our tiredness and the failing light.

Dithering about for a while longer, Murray turned for the bivvy rock, deciding to leave the animals until dawn. But for some reason in those hundred metres back to camp he summoned the energy and suddenly it was all on; so we hurriedly grabbed gear like ammo, knife, first-aid pouch and headlamp.

Skirting the bush on the true right we soon entered a finger of bush that we reckoned would bring us out in a belt of ribbonwood and crown fern, wherein we could sneak in on the bull for a better look. We gained ground surprisingly quickly and occasionally snuck a peek with the binoculars to see what the bull was up to. Soon enough, we spotted a cow feeding below the bull and then I spied an extra set of antlers in the hollow where the animal was holed up.

Now this set of antlers looked a lot wider, and the stakes suddenly changed as we manoeuvred closer under the camouflage of the thick undergrowth. We just couldn't see the bigger animal clearly and only occasionally would the original bull step up out of his hollow for a look around. He certainly was a large-sized animal and we were close enough now to be counting points. The half-light of twilight made this difficult, though, and at each fading moment that the bull did give opportunity for us to glimpse his antlers we just got confused even more. We felt pretty sure we were looking at a 10-pointer of very good length but not such a good spread — especially when we matched that with the few frontal glimpses we got of the larger rack on the hidden beast.

At 150 metres we paused for some time, waiting for a decent view. Murray was ready just in case, with his rifle rested in the V of a ribbonwood branch. Time ticked by with no favours granted by the larger beast. We were being wise and trying hard to protect some of the efforts of the Wapiti Foundation in restoring this herd, yet at the same time it's the animals themselves who also fight to survive. We knew crafty bulls such as this could still grow old in these hills and our threat was a healthy and natural part of the maturing of such great bulls. Finally, with a decisive turn, Murray gave it away as blackness overtook the last light-gathering capabilities of his scope. We'd have to be in position the next morning now.

The journey back down through the ribbonwood and scrub was aided by stumbling into a dry creekbed, and with just a few spills we managed to get back to the home bush, with our adjusted night vision held off by not using our headlamps until absolutely necessary. Interestingly, as soon as we turned them on way down within the bush layer, an animal started barking from up on the headwall. They now knew we were here!

Dinner came late that night but was gobbled down by two well-tired hunters. Little did we foresee that this was to be the pattern for the next few challenging days as we continued to stretch out just how late we could eat dinner.

We ate well after our first full days. *Greig Caigou*

At first light we were up and away to check on the movements of those deer.

Back at the bush edge again we soon started seeing deer, counting five animals across the face but had some trouble picking up the bulls. With patience, though, I soon spotted one and before long we were seeing animals everywhere. In all, we counted 12 animals in terrain as varied as thick ribbonwood and scrub to open grasslands and up and down the range of altitudes. Interestingly, we found you need to keep checking over the same country several times. One hot tip for hunters new to this region would be to not assume that there aren't any animals present after a first look. Some scrub is so thick that they can be out of sight and later they just magically appear.

We could see only the one bull, however, and he was further up the rift from where he had been positioned the evening before. We felt sure the larger beast was around somewhere but we couldn't locate him.

We studied that bull for some time and ultimately believed him to be less of a bull than we'd rated him in the fading light of the evening before. We kept looking and enjoyed following animals in their morning feeding while at the same time studying the lie of the land and possible ways up onto the tops. The route via the prominent waterfall at the head of this lower basin looked best. We went back to watching the animals and it was great seeing so many out on the open tops.

At one point I noticed the bull start to gain height at a much quicker rate than his previous feeding pace and wondered: why the hurry? Perhaps he'd seen the other bull and was catching up to his mate. Soon enough, though, we heard it too and the faint 'thump thump' of a rotor crystallized in the distance. Chopper!

The deer were on the move now and, surprisingly, were climbing really quickly. But why climb?

They were congregating towards a high terrace as the unmistakable whine of a helicopter invaded the valley. As the machine came into view the animals were galloping in single file across the high snowgrass terrace, heading for a finger of bush above us. They had an established escape route and were making for it, at pace. Soon they were fleeing into the scrubby bush, but the machine flew along our ridge and into the hanging basin and seemed to fade away in that distance. We could just hear that the heli was in the head of one of the nearby valleys but it hadn't seemed to be hunting as it came through. I was surprised it was there at all, as this is a wilderness zone and, even if it hadn't landed, the noise interruption certainly took away from the experience of being there. (Even more reason to restrict landing zones and flight paths for such intrusions to wilderness areas. Despite any geological, vegetation or other such surveys, there are users of these designated regions who value and expect 'natural quiet'.)

While all this was happening I kept my eye focused on the entry point the animals had taken into the bush high up on the flanks of the basin and soon noticed another cow moving down from on high and making her escape at the same exit. She just happened to be followed by a great bull and here, I realized, was the big fella from last night. He swung his head around as he changed his descent into sidling, and in those few brief moments and in the good light of day, I knew I'd certainly spotted a truly big bull. The standout feature was the tall antlers which reached far back on his body and even seemed too big compared to his great bulk. Another attribute was the great spread, reaching wide as he turned his head around for a final look before pushing into the bushline. How good was that!

We sat there stunned at the sudden change of events of the last few minutes and before long we again heard the whine of the helicopter as it swung back into view high above the falls, straight-lining towards the Wapiti River area. It did not appear to be hunting and within moments we were left again with the peace of the mountains, albeit quiet and now 'lifeless' in contrast to the earlier scenes at dawn.

While sitting discussing the turn of events, ascent routes and how the changing weather would bear on our plans to climb for the tops, I happened to notice a movement in the trees across the river. It was a cow, picking her way out of the bush — the same finger of bush that extended all the way up to the escape route the group of animals had taken earlier.

In a snap the video camera was out and what followed was a thrilling passage of time and footage as animal after animal emerged from the bush and slowly, but purposefully, ambled across the clearing and back into the bush at another entry point further along.

What if the bulls emerged on the same line? *What if* the big fella did the same?

With adrenaline fuelling the moment, Murray set up in a good line of fire and I snuck in behind a shrub with the camera rolling as, intermittently, animals emerged from the bush in pretty much the same place as the first animal and wandered over to enter the lower bush on quite a prescribed path. It was exciting, more so for the expectation of the big bull following up behind somewhere.

Before long I noticed the movement of something emerging from a different path and then right across the head of the clearing came two bulls, as brash as could be. With no care in the world these animals straight-lined across the middle of the clearing and played merry havoc with me trying to focus the video and hold steady enough as they weaved among the scrub and transited at only 30 metres away. (I wished I'd taken time to get a better rest for the camera!)

Murray studied these bulls, but they were an eight- and a six-pointer, with one holding promise for future years in terms of antler shape, whereas the other was really narrow.

Still we waited, hearts racing as we strained our eyes into the bush looking for the big bull to emerge. It was intense … mostly because we didn't know just how big the animal would be and also because the animals didn't linger on the clearing long but instead steadily made their way over to the same entry point to the forest across the river.

We waited.

We waited for some time, especially as we understood that a bigger or older bull would take his time and would perhaps be more cautious before coming out onto open ground.

He never emerged from that bush! We kind of knew that a really big bull didn't get that way from flaunting himself in open spaces in broad daylight, and so with a decent touch of respect we finally gave up on our morning events and headed the short distance back to our rock for breakfast.

There were other days yet, other bulls out there. We knew now that big bulls had still survived all the hunting parties of other years and hope welled up in us for what could lie ahead. Perhaps there was a big bull out there that we could get the drop on?

Little did we know how true that would be!

Chapter 2

Fiordland delivers

Murray and I now knew there was a 'big fella' bull in residence in the top of the Henderson Burn, but the weather had turned, and with the temperature dropping and drizzle getting heavier we retreated to our haven under the rock in the bush.

The day dragged on into evening and a good time was spent in our bags refuelling our bodies with copious amounts of both sleep and sweet tea. Those who know will appreciate how time drags in these situations and it was almost in total contrast to how things had been for us over the last 48 hours. On the one hand, we had so much to do and so little time before leaving home in Nelson and now we had so little to do and so much time!

Of course, the subject of big bulls and a game plan got its share of airtime.

It was wholly plausible that we'd need good tactics to out-manoeuvre the large bull, and with our scent now in the headwaters it seemed prudent to move out, gain height and be in position for spotting him from above. Certainly, moving out of the bottom of the basin during the rain fitted well with one of the few tips I've picked up from more experienced hunters in the wapiti country. Get into position during the bad weather and be ready for when it clears.

We were set then on moving to a high camp during the poorer weather. The long-range forecast we'd checked prior to coming in had us set for a couple of days of cold southwesterlies and heavy rain, so we decided to settle in for the day and night and make a break for higher ground when and if the weather showed signs of easing off the next day. With that agreed, it was back to more naps under our spacious rock shelter, which was much better than being cramped in a two-man tent.

In between naps we established that I was the 'world champion' at checkers after playing it out on our pack liner using small stones for the pieces. Then it was time for more tea and I soon fell in love again with the sweet black brews. Murray is a beekeeper and it's pretty special to lace black tea with fully natural, top-of-the-range manuka honey, sourced from the pristine Marlborough Sounds. In fact, I think it's Murray's beekeeping and hive repositioning work that gives him such a good base of fitness, and he's such a good mate in terms of overall work output. Even after a hard day on foot he arrives in camp and gets straight on with the necessary chores. This is a valuable attribute in any cobber, though one downside of his workrate is that he seems more efficient than me at getting sorted and ready to go — even if he starts packing up after me!

Another likeable quirk of Murray's is that he loves his down jacket as it's such a lightweight and compact piece of clothing, ideal for the kind of colder enforced situation we were now in, where we were not moving about much. When he gets too hot in his thick sleeping bag, the jacket comes off to make a fluffy pillow. Over the ensuing hours this 'pansy' comfort came in for some ridicule until I got quite cold somewhere in the wee small hours of the morning! (In the interests of more space and a lighter pack I'd left out my down jacket and had brought my Macpac Pinnacle sleeping bag that has down only on the top.) February it may have been, but overall it was a tad cool until the northwesters arrived later in the week.

Dawn was a long time coming and the rain still soaked the forest outside our accommodation. Now, too, the cups of tea were pressing hard and there was little incentive to get out from the comforts of the rock to empty a bursting bladder. (I've often told myself at these times how useful a compacted plastic milk container would be. So light and so useful for doing your business without having to extricate yourself from the creature comforts of the sack!)

With our plan fixed we just had to wait it out, and by early afternoon there were increasing signs that the heavier rain had eased back and by the time of intermittent drizzle we were packing up and heading for the high tops.

Back at the edge of the clearing we checked in with the favoured slopes on the headwall before crossing to the waterfall and climbing up the true right face among thick growth that was woven with deer trails. This obvious route was certainly the preferred access way into the hanging basin, and in good time we sidled across to the crest of the waterfall and into a wide expanse of tussockland.

Great sodden areas told tales of deer spending plenty of time up here, but none was about today. It must have been a great sight in years gone, for those who made the effort, to see great herds of animals roaming across the faces. With plenty of open ground up here, however, they would have also been easily boxed in and some bloody slaughter inflicted.

There are some pleasant alpine tarns in this basin, and from them it's easy going to swing up to the south onto a leading spur. This runs up towards the main ridge and our goal of the low saddle back out towards the faces above where we'd spotted the big bull.

Murray pauses to enjoy the view back into the Henderson Burn. *Greig Caigou*

Travel here is good, and with mountain fitness returning to our systems Murray and I made light work of the ascent and had camp set up right under the ridgeline in good time to allow us an afternoon jaunt over towards the Edith Saddle country. Without going all the way along the ridge, we spent some good time glassing heaps of country and stretching our eyes in all directions as the weather improved to a brilliant evening.

Back above the headwall of the Wapiti River, we settled in to see what emerged from the bush as the evening wore on and the light retreated to high points before slowly dipping below the crinkle-cut skyline of mountain ranges out to the west. We watched as below us a cow and fawn boldly marched out into the centre of the expansive flats and started feeding. Suddenly, two more deer magically appeared. They must have been resting up in the middle of the day, quite invisible in the lie of the land or the thick cover.

We kept watch and loved seeing the animals pick their way up into the ribbonwood, completely invisible from below no doubt but wholly obvious to us on our high perch. This was the way to set yourself up for locating animals, and as the light grew duller I picked up movement on the bush edge far below. At this later time it was the bulls starting to appear and feed out towards the headwall. First, there was what transpired to be an eight-pointer and then later a larger set of antlers appeared hard over against the thicker undergrowth. This animal looked like a 10 and had good length to his antlers, but it was hard to see whether he had two or three points on one topside.

Darkness was all around as we made our way back along the ridge towards camp and a late dinner at 10.30. It was mighty nice sitting on our rampart with views of deep darkness dropping off below as we tucked into our meal and lingered over cups of hot tea. With stars plastering the crisp night sky, the next day held much promise and we agreed to head towards the Lugar Burn before daybreak and endeavour to catch out that big bull we were there for.

The first blush of dawn was evident out to the east as Murray and I picked our way through the rocks and up onto the ridgeline that would give us access to the ridge coming around to our right from the head of the McDougall branch of the Lugar Burn. I love those early starts, and the sense of anticipation was brisk in our steps as we started the work up the slope. Soon enough we were sidling around to gain position for glassing, and there was so much country we just didn't know where to look first.

Here we were back on familiar ground, and my binos darted from hot spot to hot spot as I scanned sites where animals had been sighted so easily in the past. Murray was having the same problem, and we kept wanting to adjust our position so that we could suck in more of the hot spots from our memory banks.

No deer were seen, so we moved further along the ridgeline and repeated the exercise at each vantage point.

Before long, though, our eyes were 'bino'd out' and we angled along to the spot where the cover photograph for my first book had been taken. It was especially neat to be there, to be back, taking in all those now familiar vistas. Out to the north lay the blue jewel of the lake at the head of Wapiti River, with its ribbon of water cutting down into the head basin we'd spied the bulls in the evening before. We could look all the way down into Wapiti River to Lake Sutherland and all the country in each of the side basins over there. Along the ridge the slope climbed easily up towards the head of Canyon Creek while, swinging and gazing southeast, the long and familiar valley of the Lugar reached back towards Te Anau.

With just a few cows spotted in the head of the Lugar we set off up the ridge towards the Canyon Creek watershed. Suddenly, Murray ducked down with that sense of something spotted ahead. With some motions of his fingers above his head I got the message that he'd spied a bull and quickly unhitched my pack to grab the video camera.

We peeked up over the rise as Murray gave me directions to the animal. It took a wee while for me to pick out the deer, but a movement much closer than where I'd been looking soon had me on target. The wind was wafting along behind us and now the bull was on the move as I got the recording button working and zoomed in on the now departing eight-pointer. It was great to have the film rolling as the bull climbed steadily above us and finally paused on the skyline before giving his head a couple of turns to show off his average antlers against the vivid blue of the skyline.

We were surprised at just how high this bull was out on the tops at mid-morning, but it reflected my new friend Jansen's observations that red deer stags get high up in late summer prior to the roar. The same is no doubt true for wapiti. Of course, the animals are where you find them, and we continued that day checking all types of terrain and straining our eyes as we glassed great expanses of country during our progress above Canyon Creek and the Lugar. Animals were spotted bedded down during the middle of the day, and way over on the other side of the Lugar Burn a good number of cows fed out of some rocky slopes in the mid-afternoon. This had been the hideaway area for the big bull we were seeking and we resolved to get into that area another day.

Above Canyon Creek — a glorious day in Fiordland. *Greig Caigou*

Naturally, we took time out during the middle of the day to have a siesta and to hatch plans for the rest of the day. It seemed best to return to our camp site, have an early dinner and then descend to Wapiti River to a good vantage point and await the reappearance of the bulls we'd spied the evening before. We wanted to check out the larger of those beasts, and with the plan agreed we eventually turned for home along the ridge and the climb back around into the saddle.

A dinner of classic beef curry from Back Country products was supplemented with some Uncle Ben's boil-in-the-bag rice and copious amounts of tea before we grabbed our gear and dropped down over the ridge to set up our ambush. Keeping our eyes on the scrubby country, we manoeuvred around down the slopes on the true right of the gully, taking advantage of the thick growth there. Our aim was to get low and be in good range to cover the expanse of flats which led up to the rock and scrub level that the bulls had fed into the evening before.

Then the waiting began as we kept vigil. The glare of the day gradually subsided as long shadows ascended the slopes, chasing beautiful rich colours before them. I have come to love this evening light at low angles, and it was a wonderful closing to the day that had begun high above, 15 hours earlier, as we'd set out in the pre-dawn to get into viewing position on the main ridge.

We were very well concealed in the slot of a small stream, with high hebes and alpine grasses all about and with good views over all the country the animals had emerged from the evening before. Nothing was showing this evening, however, as the last of that day's light touched the high peaks off to the west. Where were they? Keeping watch, we focused more and more on the bush edge now, as this was where we expected the bulls to ease into view … if indeed they planned to be feeding out tonight in those last twilight moments.

Feeling somewhat cramped, I switched positions to move a few metres lower down the creekbed and poked my head up again to scan the overgrown faces below, which stretched across towards some nearby bush.

Immediately, I picked up movement as tall antlers swung about among scrub 50 metres below me. In a flash I realized the bull had been out of the bush for ages and was here on our side of the slopes and had been feeding in the lush growth all that time.

Frantic moments followed as I alerted Murray while slithering back from my perch with a sense of urgency. Light was fading fast as we each scrambled for position: Murray to find a shooting stance and me to get the video camera set up as quickly as possible. Out of the corner of my eye I could see Murray trying to get a rest in one spot before giving up on that and rearranging himself a few metres further down the creek. He was trying to get a good rest with his rifle perched across a branch of scrub. Meanwhile, I zoomed out and in with the camera several times, trying to locate the animal in the viewfinder before zooming in to close range. The light was low and I knew Murray would be assessing whether to take the wapiti or not, while I was desperately trying to capture some decent footage before any shot. Suddenly, the excitement and scatter of those last moments was shattered as a shot exploded away.

Through the viewfinder I saw the bull wince as he took a hit then leap forward across the slope. He was on the move and immediately I dropped the camera to the grass and grabbed my binoculars to follow the animal as it galloped over the thick scrub towards the bush. When it went down I needed to have a keen eye on its whereabouts. Another shot rang out from the .308 and the bull slumped forward, thrashing about as it tumbled into a hollow just before the bush.

My glasses were still on it as Murray hit the animal again and we both watched for several moments hoping it was down for good.

It wasn't long before we were alongside the fallen animal and Murray proudly lifted aloft the antlers of his first wapiti bull. This was a very strong 10-point animal with solid beam, long length and very respectable spread, and Murray was as pleased as punch. The 10 points took nothing at all from the rack and the head was a very good reward for someone from Nelson who had done the hard yards, seized the opportunity from our game plan and taken a good specimen to remember our journeys in this magnificent area.

As a team we quickly set about removing the head and grabbing the backsteaks and heart, while I also cast glances up the hill to fathom the best ascent route before the darkness completely enveloped the headwall. The meat, along with both our sets of gear, were bundled into my pack as Murray hoisted the antlers onto his shoulders and we set off up the slope with me route-finding and Murray putting in the effort with the bulk of the antlers.

The climb was steady, but surprisingly our legs were in good shape given the long day we'd had on foot. We pushed on up, using a creekbed to save bashing through any scrub, and finally emerged on the easier going of the open snowgrass at around 10 p.m. Soon enough we were descending the short section to our camp site on the opposite side of the ridge. It was a magical feeling to walk into camp with great dark chasms falling away below our little terrace, zillions of stars above and the weariness of a successful hunt upon our shoulders.

We'd been hunting for 16 hours from pre-dawn until after dark and had taken in some great scenery, some tense and exciting moments as well as putting in some hard work to achieve the satisfaction of meat and antlers back at camp, and all the while had watched over 15 animals in the wild. As well we were starting to feel that oneness with our environment and the return of mountain fitness to our bodies.

That night we chose to sleep under the stars way out there on that ridge top. I lay looking up to the wonders of the Milky Way, soaking in the specialness of it all as the eyes grew weary and sweet sleep settled over me. Magic stuff.

A new day woke me just on first light and what a sight greeted me as I turned to look over towards the glow in the east. A great veil of white fog lay in the valley below and as this was tinged with the colours of dawn I jumped out of the bag and reached for my camera to capture the scene. Of course, that activity brought new life to my system and once fired up I resolved to don my boots, grab my rifle and binos and drop down the slope to check for the big Henderson bull we'd seen earlier.

I left Murray grabbing some extra zeds and dropped to a vantage point to begin my searching of all the likely spots under the rimrock. It was quite distracting putting my eyes to the binoculars because the dawn was unfolding beautifully around me with ever-changing hues reflecting off the higher rock buttresses and alpine grasslands while the valley fog provided the covered contrast below. I was intoxicated with Fiordland as I took all this in and loaded it into memory banks already brimming from the full day and the magic night just past.

I was there as much for the experience of the wilderness all about me as for the searching out of wild game. In between appreciating the wider glory of that morning I allowed some zooming in on features that were taking shape in the amphitheatre below me. Constantly, I refocused from wide angle to microscopic, as my attention swung from the majesty of the mountains in macro to scanning the slopes in minute detail, looking for deer.

Soon it was time to get back up to Murray as the big Henderson bull was not apparent. (In the subsequent ballot period I'm sure this Henderson bull was the one that fell to an Australian hunter and turned out to be carrying a decent 40-inch-plus set of antlers.) As I climbed back into camp I was greeted with the strong smells of fresh wapiti heart and dehy onions fried in oily butter. Add a hot cuppa and a rock bench with million-dollar views and life seemed pretty good for us up there on the tops that morning!

After a leisurely set of second and third helpings of fried heart we resolved to fill a light pack and make for a fly camp over towards the Edith Saddle area. Without much fuss we were soon on our way, cutting up the narrow ridge and along the highest tops in easy time. Fitness was building and our legs were now working as they should. Mind you, the lighter packs sure helped and before long we were overlooking the Midnight Creek basin and sussing out likely camp spots from on high.

We decided to leave our packs and stretch out along the spur a short distance just so we could catch a view down into the upper Glaisnock. Our plan was to return later to set up camp and have a snooze before another evening vigil above Midnight Creek and the Edith Saddle. Leading along the spur it was very easy going, and at one point I got a whiff of deer. I checked in with Murray and he verified the same so I eased the pace and took on more caution as each new view unfolded ahead of me. At one point I was a bit ahead of Murray when a low whistle had me spin about to see Murray excitedly motioning me back up the slope.

Deer disturbed on the tops. *Gordon Max*

Immediately, I retraced my steps, as I knew by his manner that he'd spotted something of consequence! Sure enough he'd managed to detect a different colour in the rockfall off to the side of the spur and there, right in among the rocks, was a resting bull — and what's more there were antlers showing some promise!

Who would have believed it? The bull was way out of the bush, just under the main ridgeline and sleeping among the rocks in the middle of the day. We were undetected at 200 metres and so set about wriggling into position and getting a good rest for the video camera while we studied the bull. It was unclear just how many points the beast had because he wasn't moving his head about. Instead, the bull lay motionless, resting while high above we tried several angles to get a fix on the number of points. I even used the camera's extra optical zoom to see if I could distinguish the exact number, but the clarity through the viewfinder was insufficient.

Finally, we resolved that he was at least an 11-pointer as it was clear he had three good points on each top, but because of the positioning of his head we were not sure whether he had the necessary bez tine on one antler. It was to be my shot, if I wanted to take it — and for a long time I felt I wouldn't take the shot. I pondered the carry-out that I knew from experience was the harder part of shooting a bull in this country. I also wondered whether this was a bull that should be left to grow older and bigger for future hunters. I knew, too, that I could not take the meat and so I had time to ask myself if I was prepared to lay a big beast down just for a set of antlers.

You see, I'd faced the aftermath of such a shot before!

I had plenty of time.

I thought of getting closer for a more thorough check on the antlers, but the shooting platform was very good where I lay so I was a little reluctant to give that up for perhaps a less steady position if I crept in. Meanwhile, I took some video footage of the animal as it lay basking in the sun, even if it was a little ordinary because of no real movement.

Eventually, though, Murray pressed me for what I was going to do, and once nudged I decided to take the wapiti and so closed down the bolt. I settled in behind the butt of the .270 much like at the shooting range that I'd spent some time at, back at Cable Bay in Nelson. The target was steady for sure and my hold just in behind his shoulder was rock solid as I squeezed off.

The impact thumped back to us high above and with that the animal just tilted over more into the rocks. The shot was good but I held on the bull just in case. He was thrashing his head about a bit and was trying to paw at the ground with his front feet so I sent another 150-grain projectile on its way just to be sure and with that the deed was done.

With mixed feelings of elation at a good shot made but with a doubted decision, I set off down the hill as Murray went off to gather up knives and the other camera from the packs we'd left back along the ridge.

Approaching the bull I was already feeling some unease and the great beast was collapsed in among the rocks heaving his chest as the life drained out of his body. I sat down below him, almost face to face — but I felt shamed in my own presence.

It hurt!

It hurt because today I'd made a call to fire when pretty much all that was within me had resolved on a previous trip not to pull the trigger on such a great beast this far into a wilderness area. It just seemed such a waste to cut down a wapiti bull for the sake of some antlers only (even if it was a good 11-pointer with solid beam and strong lower tines). It's just too hard to bring all that meat out of Fiordland or at least I'd have to be prepared to do so!

In that moment I knew all interest in 'antlers' was gone for me now. Perhaps I'd come full circle in my stalking adventures and was returning to a foundational position of killing just for meat.

High above the Glaisnock with the bull that caused me grief. *Greig Caigou*

But I loved the hunting. I really love the adventure of it all and the Fiordland environment is just superb in providing the essential ingredients I need. I love being there and I loved seeing the animals. So I guessed the camera would have to be my stalking challenge and 'rush' on future trips in this area. For the longest time, I truly felt like I'd shot and killed my last bull wapiti here.

For me, though, the camera doesn't quite complete the essence of the hunting cycle or the connectedness with natural processes that I believe in. Spanish philosopher José Ortega y Gasset said: 'Real hunting requires the death of the animal, or at least the possibility of the death of the animal, because it authenticates the entire procedure and grounds it in reality.'

I would still shoot to kill and I will still shoot stags, but they will be closer to home in areas that I'm prepared to carry all the meat out from. And if I carry my rifle back into this part of Fiordland I know there will be that much stronger resolve to put in the extra effort in terms of carrying out all the meat. This is now such a trophy herd that if I ever change my mind in future and consider shooting a mature bull I would have to get past some very strongly felt boundaries that I've placed upon myself. In those moments alone with the bull I resolved to not let myself down again in terms of the personal values I have been trying to uphold.

It must be remembered, though, that it does take time for any hunter to arrive at their own parameters for shooting an animal and this must be especially considered in the education of those who venture into Fiordland among this heritage herd of wapiti.

Notwithstanding this personal code, I was not about to judge or inflict my creed upon my hunting mate, and so Murray and I discussed my resolve as we set about removing the head and the two massive backstraps of dark meat that would come home with me.

After a short pitch back up to the ridge top I stowed the antlers and we set off back along the spur to drop down to the area where we proposed to fly camp. Soon enough, we'd sorted a good space out of view of the country below and tight in a sheltered depression, in case of wind. One of the disadvantages with fly camping is that it's nice to have the fly pitched high for a little headroom, but if this is too high the wind gets underneath and billows the nylon up like a parachute wing. Of course, if the wind is gusting, this puts tremendous strain on the seams and fixing points and a hunter's camp can quickly get shredded. One way to reduce the strain on fly camps is to pitch them low out of the wind and to use segments of light bungee cord at the guy ropes to absorb any sudden stresses from wind gusts.

We snoozed through the mid-afternoon sun and then repeated our strategy of an early dinner before gathering up basic kit and moving downslope to find some suitable spotting place. Here we lingered well into the evening, frequently checking over all the likely slopes and searching among the clearings in the bush fringes as well as the nooks and crannies of thick vegetation around the valley headwall. It certainly was big country in the Edith Saddle area, and I frequently took my concentration from out of the Leupold binoculars so as to study the expanses of country I had read about.

Off to my right the upper Glaisnock Valley swung into its North Branch and we could see where a great cleft ran down into the valley floor right from the top of the spur leading up from Edith Saddle. That spur was the obvious route up, angling left to cross over above Lake Oilskin and the pass of the same name. All that country was in very easy reach now and we hoped it would see us back in subsequent years. Far off to the west the clouds had been thickening and mountain peaks jutted into the entire skyline with all manner of shapes, ranging from the tidy symmetry of Overhead Cone to convoluted crags and mighty monoliths dotted all along the Darran Mountains in the far distance.

We also kept watch over all the territory below as the evening wore on and darkness again settled around us. Surprisingly, the whole scene seemed devoid of game and neither bulls nor cows were located that evening. We knew, however, that they had to be there somewhere and so we tarried until darkness set in before turning and stepping up the hill to our warm bags. Some light drizzle began to carry through on the breeze from the approaching front.

Sleep came easy in our wee haven and morning revealed a pool of water in a sag of the fly immediately above my head. Easing up on the nylon I chased the pool away to spill off a corner of the fly and amused myself for some time watching drops form into rivulets and then flow into each other to amass greater drops of water as yet another pool built itself in the sag of the nylon.

We dozed in and out of sleep as drifts of rain or drizzle came through the upper valley and around mid-morning we sensed a lighter sky as we gazed out from underneath our shelter. In time the light was even brighter and we unkinked our bodies enough to venture out in bare feet for a leak and to check on the situation.

A magnificent Fiordland morning greeted us as blue sky began to burn into view between billows of mist funnelling up from Midnight Creek below. All around us was the freshness of the rain mixed with this new and brighter day that was trying to burst out from the moisture rising up past our camp site. We stood in the middle of the layer between blue sky above and mist below and as each billow came through we caught fleeting glimpses of the sun-speckled slopes beneath us. With the promise of a good day on the way Murray donned his boots and grabbed his gear as I busied myself trying to capture these Fiordland moments from interesting camera angles!

We emerged from our high camp to clearing weather. *Greig Caigou*

During this time I realized my battery life was coming to an end and so I made the most of what was left. Murray meanwhile had dropped down to a hummock where he could look over the upper Midnight Creek area whenever an opportunity presented itself through the mist. The mist thickened up and he was left alone in a world of white and zero visibility for quite some time, so I put on another brew while waiting for his return.

After half an hour Murray finally materialized from the mist and I checked in as to whether he managed to get much of a view below and whether any animals were out and about. He'd not got many chances to glass the valley but had seen one bull, so it was good to know there were animals in the area after having drawn a blank the evening before.

We had our tea and some breakfast and as the weather was improving set about hanging out our sleeping and bivvy bags for an airing. With the better visibility we wandered down to a vantage point to check in on the bull Murray had spotted.

The animal was feeding hard in against a rock gulch that was choked with ribbonwood at its base and totally invisible from below. However, from our viewpoint Murray had been able to catch him moving about in the security of the misty whiteout, and now that he was settling in against the gulch he would have been very difficult to discover.

Once Murray had detailed where to find him I focused in on the little gulch and as soon as I picked up the bulk of the animal I knew we were looking at a monster bull!

'Murray, that's a great head ... look at the spread of that thing!'

The more we looked the more we knew we were looking at a class wapiti. We watched and watched and it was great to see his huge size and wide antlers swing about as he tore off foliage to munch on.

Initially, when Murray had spotted the animal he'd considered it as just another good bull, but as we concentrated on the bull the more Murray came to appreciate what he had been looking at. For one thing, as the antlers reached up from his head to the trez tines they took a step outwards, greatly increasing the spread, easily beyond the girth of the animal. Periodically, the bull reached up to feed off the wall of his hideaway and then the length of antler was even more obvious from above.

What was not clear to either of us was the number of points. Murray had determined he wasn't going to shoot another bull unless it held more points than the one he'd already taken. There was no point in being greedy and Murray was fully happy with his memento from this trip. However, there was a certain bulk to this head that I considered outweighed any number of 'points' and if Murray wanted a true trophy head from the wapiti country I suggested this was it. Murray was still hesitant.

'I'm with you if you want to shoot it, Murray. I'll carry out the two other heads so you can manage that one if you want.'

'Let's get in closer so that we can check the points then,' Murray added, and with that we retreated to our nearby camp site to gather up all that we would need for the stalk.

Battery life on the digital SLR was all gone so it was the video camera I grabbed. I put in a few seconds of footage from the high point in case our bull was to disappear and it was then I noticed there was only 1.5 metres of tape left. Not enough to record any of the proceedings! So we stalled for a bit while I rewound through the last sequences of the bull and the clearing mist at our camp site in order to gain some more tape. I then added back in another very short sequence of the bull with the zoom on maximum.

Now we were off, down through a cutting we had determined would keep us out of sight until we made the flat going across the basin floor. That crossing would still be in sight of the animal, but we figured we could manage that obstacle when it came.

Approaching this section, I noticed another drift of fog coming up from the valley below so with a quick wink at Murray I bolted across the grasslands, making for a large rock as quickly as I could to take advantage of the handy cover of the mist. What a bonus! We were now around 200 metres from the bull, which had bedded down in his hideaway. All we could see was the top of his head and that massive rack of antler standing tall like the branches of a bush.

We spent some time studying the tops of each antler because from above we'd thought the tops didn't looked formed or else were still shredding velvet, which had made it hard to make out any points. However, from our position now, the animal was face on and this task was no easier. What was clearly apparent, though, was the bulk of the antlers and the great spread.

Murray was undecided but knew a decision had to be made and as we discussed the ramifications of a shot it gradually became apparent that he wanted to take the shot.

With that sorted we settled in, to play a waiting game for a better target to present itself. For this we needed the bull to stand up and so we propped in behind the rock with Murray set up with a perfect rest. I grabbed some extra footage at this range and then we waited. And we waited ... and then waited some more, taking turns to report in on any sign of movement so that Murray would be steady for the shot. But nothing stirred.

The wapiti had gone off to sleep and was holding fast in his little lair.

This is how old bulls survive in the wapiti country. Here was a cunning old bull that had learned where to put himself out of harm's way over many years. Any approach from below would have had this bull scenting the approaching danger, after which he could quietly merge into the ribbonwood stand. For all those who passed, it would seem nothing was about. There had been many hunting parties into the Edith Saddle area over the years but clearly a remnant of sizeable beasts had survived. Also these old fellas are more at ease when under cover of rain, cloud or darkness. Presumably, this bull had been one of those making all the sign we observed out on the slopes but had possibly been doing this under cover of the elements before retreating to his hideaway. The fact of our being prepared to camp out on the high ground in the poor weather and to be out of bed, on hand, at the first sign of a clearance is part of the mix that increases a hunter's luck. (In fact the same could be said of our good fortune with the plan from a few days earlier, where we'd been prepared to hold a stakeout until after dark, knowing that we'd be climbing to our beds well into the night.) Effort brings reward.

After some considerable time we started to reassess our plan. Murray just needed the animal to stand up, and as I was keen to get some more video footage it seemed probable that I could sneak in for some closer filming while Murray held on the animal at his good bench rest. The plan meant that if at any stage the bull was alarmed or showed signs of fleeing, Murray could send the shot on its way. I didn't want Murray to be disadvantaged in any way by my attempt to get some footage.

So with this firmly agreed between us I slipped my Huntech gillie cape over my head, checked the camera and set off at an angle towards another small rock. Upon checking on the animal again it all appeared good so I began a stalk that allowed me to take advantage of lines behind rocks to hide me. Periodically, I had to crawl over patches of rough ground and shimmy over small rocks, but all the time I was closing the gap and each new check-in on the bull showed him still motionless in his hideaway. Asleep … I thought.

Later I was to learn that Murray stayed fixed in position and every now and then would check in on my progress from where he'd seen me prior. He mentioned the alpine pattern camouflage was working so well that he'd had real trouble finding me again; it would be just a flicker of movement that would give my location away. I knew, too, that the stalk was going well and I found my heart racing as the gap closed down to around 50 or so metres. This stalk with the video camera was proving every bit as exciting as if I'd held a rifle and when I eased out from beside a rock I was able to zoom right in on the eyes of the quarry — and he was looking straight at me!

Squeezing the record button, I fired a shot of precious footage and then eased back. That was intense!

I felt sure I could get closer yet and try with a better angle from higher up the slope so that I could get in more of the animal and with scenery in the background. With that goal in mind I angled my crawl upslope. Just then all my focus was blasted into another realm as Murray's gunfire echoed all around.

In an instant I was up and eyes scanning the area where the bull had been. I caught a glimpse of fleeting movement as the great beast lurched forward down the gulch, crashing headlong into the ribbonwood grove. I raced forward, all the while focused on the one spot in the ribbonwood where I'd seen him keel forward. There was no bashing of undergrowth further down, no parting of the way ... and I knew he was down.

I raced carefree over the remaining rough ground and into the gulch, taking in all the hoofmarks and dollops of shit in this well worn and slippery dampness. As I sprinted around the last corner to the ribbonwood thicket there he was: all crashed down in one sprawling heap; the monarch was down. Dead.

The old bull had leapt from his familiar lair and had stumbled the last remaining paces to crash into the sanctuary of the thicket where he'd avoided many hunting parties of the past. What a great sight. Here was a great-grandfather of wapiti bulls, old and tired and finally at rest. Yes! With that, I let out a mighty 'Woo-hoo' for Murray who had scampered around his slope to be in position for any further shot should the bull bash on down through the thicket.

The bull turned out to be a whopper with thick, heavy antlers spreading out to 42 inches wide and stretching a tape measure out to 42 inches in length before stopping at the snubbed out upper points. (These upper points on both sides might have suffered during an accident in the velvet, but the more considered opinion is that the bull was so old that he had just failed to grow these out and was past his prime. We only marvelled that if the upper points had formed as normal he would have easily topped 50 inches in length!)

Murray's big wapiti bull (photo cut from video footage). *Greig Caigou*

When Murray laid eyes on the 12-pointer crashed down in the thicket, all he could manage to say was, 'Wow! ... Awrr ... Wow!'

We both stopped there for some time, taking in the broad backdrop to this scene and all the flushes of respect we felt for this old bull in his personal hideaway. He'd obviously been using this secret spot for a long time and it had worked very well for him; he'd grown old over many years in this Glaisnock wilderness area.

We made sure we took in all of the moment, before struggling to heave the old beast out into a better position so that the last precious seconds of video footage could record the monarch with his country as the backdrop.

Truly, this was a classic hunting moment for us both.

For me the trip into Fiordland that year was about a curious and special brew of mighty country and big views combined with physical and mental endurance down in the tangles of rock and sodden bush, with heavy packs on the way in and cumbersome antlers on the way out! The mix also required long days that begin in the surreal calm of pre-dawn darkness and end, wearily, in that same darkness atop the headwalls of glacial valleys with the great canopy of starlit night above. The mix has to contain seeing animals in the wild, hunting 'fair-chase', and I have to absorb the wild in some way as a hunter, at home in these places, comfortable with living and moving there in all conditions — fit and physical.

It was also about that classic image burned into my memory as Murray strode into the Fiordland skyline with that old and chunky rack of antlers tied over his pack. This was real stuff, authentic and representative to me of wilderness hunting adventures.

Memories earned.

Memories made.

Memories treasured.

Memories that need to become the reality for those who venture there after us!

Heading for home — we'll return. *Greig Caigou*

Chapter 3

Gordon Max — to hear the mighty wapiti bugle

I'd just come back from sitting down with Gordon Max in his home under the hills at Brightwater and I now had a strong and growing sense of responsibility. I knew I had just met with an absolute gentleman in every respect, an 'old school' gentleman who was both a hunter and a man to be admired in so many ways. But as I sat to write this chapter I knew I couldn't do full justice to even one classic hunting story let alone represent the full measure of this person; yet I know Gordon himself, in his own humble manner, would think he is not so special and would just tell me to do my best.

I had approached Gordon after I'd come to know of him via his son Laurence and his wife Suzanne. They run Stonehurst Farm and a horse-trekking business at Max's Bush on the terraces above the Wairoa River on the plains of Tasman Bay in Nelson. The Maxes' farm now supports a fifth generation on the land. Laurence had proudly shown me his dad's trophy red deer stag one day and recounted how he'd flown his father up into the headwaters of the Noisy Creek area in the Whitcombe region so that they could revisit the old haunts that Gordon had hunted over so many years earlier. My attention was immediately captured when I learned that Gordon had hunted over country to which many of the pioneers of stalking from Nelson had made pilgrimages. Here was a man who had known prominent Nelson stalkers Newton McConochie, Gordon Atkinson, the Shuttleworth brothers — all the names that had inspired me through their writings in my formative years as a hunter.

I wanted to meet him. I wanted to hear some of his tales and I felt an urge to revisit some of his hunting adventures and record them for that same purpose of inspiring another generation.

I had been informed that Gordon's health was failing and being in his eighty-seventh year he would not be able to talk for long. I boldly summoned the courage to ring him and set up an appointment. The phone call confirmed to me he was a frail older man, but he was happy to meet if I could keep my visits short. He knew well the limits of his energy and, besides, there were still chores he felt responsible for around the farm!

When Gordon came to the door I was greeted by a tall man and I immediately recognized the strong physical features passed through to Laurence and his youngest son Johnny who I had taught at high school, way back in a past life. I was led through to the kitchen table and Natalie, his wife, prepared a cup of tea and we sat down at the expansive table.

What struck me early in this conversation was that here was a true man of the land, with weathered hands and features that also hinted at the great strength of earlier years, and yet he was softly spoken, gentle and humble. He sat side by side with his wife, stroking her hand.

In 2010 Gordon's health had improved somewhat from the year before when he'd been quite unwell, and he told me emphatically what had been keeping him going.

'I wanted to do Natalie the honour of making it to our sixtieth wedding anniversary!'

(I am pleased to say he did and further goals were surpassed as well, such as the 100 year celebration of the establishment of the Max farm.)

We chatted about how a strapping young man met a young girl who was called in to help during a particularly busy harvest of peas. It was great hearing stories of their first date at the movies (a wartime documentary about the mighty Spitfire aeroplane no less; that wouldn't cut it nowadays). We talked about family, and I was able to piece together the foundations of the early farmers in Don Max, who had been the first All Black from the region, through to this modern era where diversification has seen a fencing contracting business arise alongside a horse-trekking operation aimed at tourists.

And I learnt so much more through the writings Gordon had assembled for his family record, entitled *The Good Old Days*, which was full of stories about farm life that recaptured an era of hard work and simple pleasures and the bonds that have grown up for the family around the land and its care.

During all these conversations, I caught a real sense of the genuine love these two shared and the strong sense of family they modelled. I also caught a hold of Gordon's love for the land and for his God and the thankfulness he had for a long and fully rich life.

When I got around to asking about hunting, I discovered Gordon was equally modest about his exploits in the hills.

For one, he attributes much of his hunting experience to Tracy Stratford, who took the much younger Gordon under his wing when Gordon's Uncle Laurie didn't return from the war. Laurie had been a favourite uncle and always had time for the young Gordon, taking him out on such boyhood adventures as eeling and local hunting forays. Uncle Laurie was the first to make the effort to come around and congratulate Gordon when he brought home his first haunch of venison. The respect he had for this man led to Gordon naming his own first son after Uncle Laurie.

When his uncle died the mantle of initiation into the greater outdoors life was taken up by Tracy Stratford, who was 21 years his senior and older than Gordon's father. Gordon describes their meeting.

'It was back in the early days of the war and the government had requisitioned all the firearms to redistribute them to the Home Guard. But Tracy was managing Haycock's Estate in the Aniseed Valley and because of the deer population he was allowed to keep his rifle. I was 16 at the time and I was used to going shooting a lot. So when we all lost our rifles and I knew Tracy had one, I got on my horse and rode into the Aniseed, where Tracy was living with Marion, and I said I'd heard about him having a rifle. Tracy lent me the rifle; he's always been a very generous joker. I never shot a deer, but when I took the rifle back he gave me a leg of venison out of his meat safe. He must have thought we could work together because he started inviting me into the Aniseed for morning and evening shots. One thing led to another and then he introduced me to Mt Arthur and the Flora Saddle area.'

This was to be a lifelong relationship that was forged in bush and mountain exploits spanning the next 64 years, over hunting grounds near and far. It was Gordon who delivered the reading at his old friend's funeral not long before Tracy's 101st birthday.

I felt the power of the connection between the two men as Gordon spoke with so much admiration for his old mate, and I found myself with a tear in my eye as Gordon recounted the music he requested for his old friend at the funeral. Amazingly, it was that same song my parents used to sing while driving us kids home from Wairoa back to Waikaremoana and which I spoke of with such significance in my first book, *Hunting Adventures*. That song, 'The Place Where I Worship', speaks of the stars as candles, lighting up the mountains; mountains are altars of God. It speaks also of the wide open spaces, built by the hand of the Lord.

That song had so firmly stuck in my childhood memory that I could not help but marvel at the mountains and wild places when I eventually found myself among them. It was instrumental in establishing my spiritual foundation and a lifelong call to return to the mountains whenever possible.

I think, too, that hunting adventures forge especially strong connections between men. To some extent it is a rite of passage into manhood that is being lost in our modern day world. There are traditions of initiation in many societies and men need to know that they have what it takes and they need some great adventure to be engaged in. Hunting exploits provide an ideal situation for a young man and an older mentor to journey along together as part of their development.

Gordon recounted several exploits of his and Tracy's, especially from their missions down into the Whitcombe and tributaries of the Hokitika. Together over the years they built up an impressive record of exploration, and Gordon has many of these moments recorded in his extensive slide and photograph collection.

Gordon, as a keen photographer, became the 'official' photographer for each hunting trip, as it wasn't common to take pictures in those days. Gordon built his own darkroom and did all his own processing. He carried two camera bodies and two lenses. He had a good-quality Leica camera and because his dad was Chair of the New Zealand Rugby Union and travelled overseas he had managed to get back home a 100 mm telephoto lens after a trip to Germany.

'Without being immodest I think I was the first one to get a pictorial record of our exploits. It has been the most special thing I could have done, especially back in the 1950s.'

He was a foundation member of the Nelson NZDA and was in great demand to do slide shows (even travelling beyond Collingwood to do a slide evening, which was a big distance in those days). Gordon said, 'When I spoke about the trips I'd also try to add a "spiritual talk" to show that a Christian didn't have to be a meek and mild little person who had to sit at home and never did any adventuring or anything like that.'

During our time together Gordon and I were able to look over some of his photograph collection and chat on familiar terms about many of the places we had hunted some two generations apart. These included such places as the Wilberforce, Whitcombe and Karangarua valleys as well as the local areas around Nelson like Beebys Knob and Ben Nevis, visible from the edge of the Max property. All the while, though, I was attentive for an enduring hunting memory to share in these pages and because of the underlying theme of this book such a story would also need to connect well with my own trips into the same country.

And so it was that we found ourselves almost inevitably in the wild places of Fiordland … and the heartland that is wapiti country!

Over several interviews with Gordon I have been able to piece together his memories of his first trip into this area. It was such a great treat for me to re-walk those wild places with him and his old mate and more so because I still felt the presence of those valleys and mountains from my recent trip with Murray.

What makes this a classic hunting memory for Gordon is that Fiordland was like a magnet, drawing him in. He just had to get into the big wapiti country and listen to the famous bugling. It was fulfilling that urge that he found so memorable.

Gordon picks up the story.

We first went into Fiordland in 1956, and all that was written on the map we had been given were a few names at the head of the North Fiord and then a great big area up the Glaisnock Valley that was labelled 'Unexplored'. We had only a few sketches and verbal information of what lay beyond!

Driving down with Jack Shuttleworth and Bert Spiers in the three-ton Bedford truck was a real mission. The truck had a canopy so we'd loaded in mattresses and bounced around in the back for the 24-hour drive south. We drove down through the Lewis Pass, as the Haast wasn't open at that stage, and got dropped up the lake by the *Tawera*.

Nelson hunters' first time on the tourist boat on Lake Te Anau. *Gordon Max*

The boat took hunters but was also a tourist ride, and while Jack and Bert were being dropped off all the tourists went over to that side to watch and this caused the boat to lean right over, giving everyone a big fright.

You'd be dropped over the side out from the beach and told by the skipper they'd be back in three weeks! Keeping track of time was an effort and we knew that the boat would've come back the next day if you missed the rendezvous, but if you were not there then they'd only come periodically after that until something worked out!

There were five in our party: Selwyn Irvine, the Murcott brothers Bill and Roger, Tracy Stratford and me. We'd won the Glaisnock Block, which was a much larger block in those days. In fact, we were to win a ballot in consecutive years and even got the same block! Selwyn and the two Murcott brothers hunted together so Tracy and I hunted as a team because five was too many to have in one party. We'd done a lot of tough trips together into Westland by then and worked together well. The only thing I didn't appreciate about Tracy was that he'd reckoned I was two-thirds bigger than him and so should carry two-thirds more weight! I found that a bit too hard to swallow.

Unloading at the mouth of the Glaisnock. *Gordon Max*

I'd learnt many of my bush skills from Tracy — he had a fantastic reputation as a bushman, so much so that he led Search and Rescue activities and instructed a guerrilla wing of the Home Guard, known as the Guide Platoon.

On one of our earliest trips out of Nelson to the Taramakau River, the weather was bad and we got stuck on the other side of the river from Jackson's Hotel. Overdue for almost a week, the concerned hotel proprietor had taken the licence plate number of our car and had rung the Nelson police. The police rang back and said: 'You needn't worry, that's Tracy Stratford and you can't lose that little bugger.' The two of us ended up cutting a track downstream for many miles to intercept the trans-alpine rail line.

We set up camp near the mouth of the Glaisnock River and our plan was to hunt the lower valley and go up some of the side creeks on fly camps. This was the usual way of hunting in those days anyway. We camped under oilskin-type fly sheets made up for us by a Nelson canvas maker. By this time in my hunting career I'd got better wet weather gear, as previously we'd only used the old Lami, an earlier version of the woollen Swanndri that got pretty heavy when wet.

Selwyn had been in the area earlier with Newton McConochie so had given us a bit of an idea of the type of travelling we could expect. We were pretty fit and tough anyway from the way of life we lived on the farm, especially during harvest time from September through to the end of January. The grain bags we hefted were four-bushel bags weighing 200 pounds. Ploughing behind a team of horses also got you strong, and a few weeks before a big trip I'd wear a bag filled with a bushel of grain when I was out ploughing on the hill. This would be great training for my shoulders. If your shoulders are going to chaff on you you're better out of it — you've no right to be there; you've got no recourse if you're going to be in the mountains for three weeks.

Off for a day hunt: Gordon at the back, Bill Murcott, Tracy Stratford, Selwyn Irvine.
Gordon Max

This kind of preparation also extended to our feet and boots especially, as they were going to be constantly wet. The local bootmaker in Brightwater made me up some new boots and I'd break them in around the farm. The fully nailed boots had three tricounis on the inside edge, four on the outside edge and a couple on the instep, which was important because otherwise you'd slip if you trod on a branch.

We did some fly camp trips up some of the side streams in the lower valley, getting up into the Henderson. I remember being impressed by the awesome sight and sound of the waterfall we struck soon after turning off from the main Glaisnock River. In the middle reaches everything had moss on it and you'd grab hold of it and find it would break in your hands.

Tracy led the way because he had such a bush sense. I had a better memory for the high country and getting around and we were both experts at lighting fires. We carried quite a lot of equipment because I also had my camera gear, and the most important item was the axe for getting wood for our cooking and warmth. We wouldn't have survived without an axe.

Into the Henderson Burn tops, 1956. *Gordon Max*

The basic food was rice and oatmeal and we took some curry and onion essence, which would help out in the stews of venison.

In those days you lived off the meat you shot on the hill. There wasn't a shortage of meat, but we just needed a few things to help those stews along. We also took a few raisins which would be added to rice if making it into a pudding. We had some luxuries back at the base camp, like fruitcake, rum and some chocolate, but that wouldn't last very long, of course. I also made camp bread in a billy, but I remember that turning out like a cow pat!

Venison steak and heaps of butter. *Gordon Max*

Fire lighting was such a necessary skill, especially in Westland and Fiordland, where days of heavy rain would challenge your skills. One of the foods we took was Sunshine soup powder, which came in a small waxed box. We would get all the tinder materials together for a fire and then use the wax of the box to help keep a good flame going under the tinder. Once a blaze was going we'd ensure a supply of dry wood by splitting wood with the axe and stacking it around the fire. This was a constant job around camp.

Tracy Stratford, ace bushman, on food prep. *Gordon Max*

We climbed high into the main Henderson basin, carrying a gunny bag for our day trips, which also held a billy and some tea with no milk powder. I would just have a dry pair of long johns back at the fly camp. I'd be carrying my cut-down .303, ammunition, a knife and of course my camera gear, which I put all together in a gas mask bag from the wartime years. This I kept slung around my neck for easy access.

There wasn't really any rush to be in the hunting ground at first light.

[I'd tried comparing notes with Gordon on his animal-hunting

methods but soon realized the efforts that we put into gaining position before first light and staying in the 'ambush zone' right on into the darkness were not actually relevant in his day.]

The animals stayed out on the tops all day so we would get away after a good breakfast. There was no pressure and the animals were not frightened of humans, except when scenting.

To me, deerstalking was the hard yakka, climbing up and finally breaking our way out through the alpine scrub with the mist drifting around, letting out a hopeful roar and sitting down with the glasses. You'd hear a stag roar, or a bull bugle — there's just nothing like it.

If anything looked promising we'd stalk in closer for a look. I got some really good photographs of several small groups of wapiti above the waterfall in that head basin as we made our climb to the main ridge. We had to be careful because if we fired a shot in those high basins, that would spoil it for the rest of the day. This was also right at the stage of the controversy about interbreeding in the wapiti area and so we had been told to remove reds and any inferior stags. Well, we only had about 30 rounds of .303 ammunition for the three weeks and so we had to be careful not to waste the shots.

If a shot was fired the animals would clear out of that basin, so we'd have to pull back and rest up a bit. We weren't under a time pressure as we were in there for three weeks and sometimes if a shot was fired or an animal missed out on, we'd go back to the fly camp and cook up a big stew instead! When we did shoot an animal we were always keen to eat the liver first off.

[Murray and I have also adopted this habit of these old-school

hunters and we love a quick fry-up of thin slices of heart, for example, along with some onions and butter for flavour!]

In the few days we were in the Henderson Burn we climbed right out on the high tops and looked over the other side into a great valley with a lovely lake high up in the head. We sat there for a long time, taking in all the country in every direction.

Base camp in the Glaisnock. *Gordon Max*

Back at base camp we met up with the others and exchanged stories about the country and dried out our gear. We'd have a smoke, too. I hadn't started my hunting life smoking but when around 24 years old and on wet days in Westland I would roll smokes for Tracy and over time one thing led to another and I ended up smoking, too.

Several of us would smoke a pipe, and it was 'part of the experience' in those days. I still remember Trace saying: 'Only a perfect tobacco could give a perfect smoke.'

Gordon Max. *Gordon Max*

Anyway, on this trip we forgot to take pipe cleaners and the pipe was getting a bit 'bubbly'. We had been having problems with several kea taking stuff around base camp so I got an idea of where we could get our pipe cleaner from! While Tracy attracted a kea's attention I grabbed the kea and clamped my hands over its beak and took out four wing feathers from each side which we trimmed up for cleaners of our smoking pipes.

Boy, you should've heard that kea squawk!

One of the cheeky kea was also responsible for stealing my monocular from the fireside. The monocular had misted up so I'd left it hung over the fire stay and in the morning couldn't find it anywhere. Nothing was safe if it was moveable — plates, boots, nothing. A kea in its curiosity must have hooked the leather strap. We searched and searched and never found it. We ended up thinking there's some kea in Fiordland flying around peering through that thing, with an advantage over the other birds.

I was only ever aware of it when we'd be out on the tops and the others were using binoculars and I had used the monocular. Anyway, for the rest of that trip in the Glaisnock I had no optics due to that pesky kea down at base camp.

[I asked Gordon why they hadn't figured to turn that kea into soup as well!

As an aside to this story it was interesting for me to learn that Gordon had, for most of his life, been left to fend with one eye. In his younger days he had been a bit of a 'gun nut', collecting and using anything that went off with a bang! He had decided to make his own revolver and found that a 12-gauge shotgun shell would fit nicely into a piece of three-quarter-inch pipe and so was born the barrel of his project. But, of course, this is where a little knowledge can be a dangerous thing, and although some testing was done Gordon had little knowledge of the breech pressure generated by the shell. He decided to make a second barrel and started playing around with that and interchanging them one night at a friend's house. Due to a horrible mistake he put in the barrel that wasn't quite fitting well and which had a live round in it and casually pulled the trigger!

The whole barrel blew out!

This smashed the wood stove that he'd pointed it at. The breech block flew back and left a deep gash down the side of his left eye as well as taking the full blast in both eyes. The lens had to be taken from the fatally damaged left eye. However, after several weeks in hospital it was a relief for Gordon to have the bandages removed and to discover that he had been fortunate to escape with vision recovering in his right eye. He was able to go on from the age of 16 and play rugby, do all his deerstalking while becoming a crack shot and in fact live a full life with just that one eye.]

We covered a lot of country in the time we were there.

We went into Nitz Creek for a few days' exploring and it was here that we came across two dead wapiti bulls at the base of very steep slopes. Wapiti have a habit of feeding up steep spurs and will get higher and higher following the tucker; they then get too high and when turning around can fall off such steep terrain.

Coming down out of Nitz Creek we came to the Glaisnock and it was running high. It was very gorgey there so we spent some time chopping at a tree so that it would fall across the chasm and we would have a bridge to use. Unfortunately, the tree missed its landing and didn't lodge on the other bank as we had hoped so we had to repeat the whole process before we could cross.

Because we also had a small dinghy, Selwyn later took us down through the Narrows and Tracy and I put in three or four days on the true right tops a short distance up the Lugar Burn. It was good for us to see the country at the river mouth where Newton McConochie from Nelson had camped and where he'd shot a really big bull under the cliffs around from the mouth of the Lugar Burn.

A bull photographed by Gordon. Photographers will appreciate the difficulty of this shot in the bush. *Gordon Max*

On those tops we found it easier country than what we'd been used to in Westland and could look down the valley out to the main lake. Looking west, though, into the upper Lugar tops, we could see mountains for miles and possibilities to reach into other catchments.

[Certainly, this had been the attraction for my returning to that country and I had asked Gordon whether that was what drew him back for more adventures in the area.]

We were bitten well before that!

In 1946 Tracy and I broke the first passage into Noisy Creek in the Whitcombe, which was a hard trip. There were no deer there, but we saw sign of some summer grazing. In 1948 we returned there because Tracy figured that by then it would be more heavily populated. That is when Tracy shot his big stag, which can be read about in Bruce Banwell's book, *The Red Stags of the Rakaia*.

Those days in the rugged Westland ranges and stalking large stags had fully taken hold of me in the previous 10 years. The trip into the Glaisnock wilderness and those side valleys only further cemented my keen interest and passion for the high country. Of course, we'd also learnt to respect the mountains by then as well. You have to respect the mountains: *If you show that respect then the mountains would respond and give you the thrill.*

Our main foray, though, was up to the famous Cave Rock camp in the Glaisnock where we set up another base. We set about drying our gear in the same way and also used some beech poles to make a drying frame. I used to tell people later that those poles were for holding up the rock!

I remember making my bed well back under the rock where I was really close to the ceiling. I woke up in the night to answer a call of nature and when I turned on my torch I got a real fright because the whole ceiling directly above me was covered with giant cave wetas.

A happy crew at the already famous Glaisnock rock bivvy, 1956. *Gordon Max*

Later we went up into the left branch of the Glaisnock and the Edith Saddle to fly camp and so ventured even further afield from there. In our next trip into this block we went straight to the Cave in the upper Glaisnock and hunted from there. We used supplies we picked up from an air drop onto the Edith Saddle.

I loved that Edith Saddle country — it has so many memories for me still!

The saddle opens up so much other country to you. I didn't know where it all went or the names of the valleys at that time.

Gordon waves his hat for joy at finding the air drop on the Edith Saddle. *Gordon Max*

[I recall just that same sense as Murray Elwood and I sat one balmy evening high above Midnight Creek looking down onto the Edith Saddle. Lifting my eyes, I could take in all the lands beyond that just leapt out of pages from the books I'd read. There were the travels of John Anderson in The Eye of the Hunter *and the stories from Allan Harrison, Ray Tinsley and many others. I could visualize the easy walk from the Edith up the spur and around and over into Oilskin Pass, for example — a name synonymous with all the great adventuring of the past. I knew that place would call me back, and so it was a dream come true to get into all that famous country early in 2011.]*

A very special memory there was a full moon night, a jolly old morepork was calling over and over again and I was sitting out taking it all in when this great feeling of 'homesickness' came over me, for want of a better word.

I said to myself, 'Gordon, what the hang are you doing here? With Natalie at home with all those children, you've no right to ...'

In looking back I see a certain selfishness about me and sometimes if you spend too much time away in the hills you get to a point when you say, it's time to go home now. But we couldn't go home like you can nowadays.

I shot my first-ever bull wapiti in that country heading back around from the left of the Edith Saddle.

The bull was a scraggy, narrow 10-pointer and didn't look like it was ever going to make a breeding animal, so we shot it for meat. I never brought the head out and we weren't going to shoot a trophy unless we saw something really special.

Tracy and I went down to Lake Alice from the Edith and also did another fly camp up onto the tops to a low point which we assumed would look over into the George River. It was to be in this area where two really special moments occurred for me, both of which I caught on camera.

We saw a big bull and Tracy told me to get my camera ready. When I was set, Tracy snapped some wood and the beast came closer. Then he'd snap the wood again. Still the bull approached and I got three photos as it came in and the last photo was with the bull almost on top of us! Tracy didn't shoot the animal, though.

Later I stalked in on another animal in that country. He was a very good bull.

When Tracy had shot the big stag in Noisy Creek we both reckoned the headskin must have weighed 50 pounds and then there were the heavy antlers as well. Because of this, I felt a bit 'intimidated' by the thought of the carry out if I'd shot this one good bull. We would've had to drop off into the Edith from above the George, then get up the Edith, over the saddle, down to the rock camp and then all the way back out to the lake. It just seemed such a mission ... so I never shot the big bull. I took a photo of him instead.

The big bull in the George. Gordon never shot him with a rifle. *Gordon Max*

[That photo still hangs proudly in his wee den at home where Gordon and I sat talking about all this wonderful country — the

old hunter and the keen and now more enlivened middle-aged man!]

I wish I had shot it now.

Possibly.

On a subsequent trip down in the Edith River we were trying to break out onto the George Saddle tops. We had a rough camp and there I experienced the most violent electrical storm I've ever been in. As usual, we would count the seconds between lightning and thunder, but at this time they came simultaneously, striking and rolling up and down the valley. We were right in the middle of it; the darn thing would go booming down-valley and then turn around and come back up again. Torrential rain thrashed all around us. I was frightened.

We only ever did two trips into the wapiti country, but they were three weeks at a time so that is probably more time than a lot of people have spent there anyway. I never shot a trophy bull wapiti with my rifle but I have those wonderful photos and memories of all that glorious country.

As I mentioned earlier, Gordon has his own written record about 'the good old days' and some of his life on the farm property which he recorded for his family and grandchildren. It is significant to me that on the last page of that record Gordon has a picture of himself as a young man and his Uncle Laurie freshening up beside a mountain tarn near St Arnaud, Nelson Lakes. Those special moments and formative years with his uncle led to a lifelong love affair with the wild places of the South Island. Gordon went on to explore far and deep into the mountains with his rifle, camera and hunting mate Tracy Stratford for many, many years. To these men he modestly showed his respect and appreciation in our many chats together in the little den at Max's Bush. You get to form really strong bonds with a hunting cobber when you've toughed it out in the challenging environments of Westland, South Westland and Fiordland that Tracy and Gordon experienced. There is no escaping the struggles of getting on with it and together facing up to the immediate consequences of living and moving in harsh environments over several weeks. That friendship was forged in wild places and grew deep because of their shared adventures and the challenging paths trodden together.

Gordon in time endeavoured to bring that same mentoring and support to others via his lifelong involvement with the Deerstalkers Association, helping out other hunters and also ensuring his own children came to have memorable outdoor experiences with their dad. Fishing trips with his daughters became a fond family memory for them, and Gordon took the boys hunting, too, even though he didn't do any more killing himself.

Most interesting for me was that the last pages of Gordon's memoirs highlight another relationship that was similarly forged over a long period of time and tested in the furnace of life as well as being so much more strengthened by times of personal reflections out in the wilderness.

That was Gordon's strong Christian faith.

Gordon remembers back to the war years and how he was confronted with so much death in the world and how this was brought home personally as five other young men went off to war from his small community along Haycocks Road, where there were just four homes in that one mile. Five went and three came back.

Gordon with his big 14-point red stag from the Mungo in Westland. *Gordon Max*

Having gone to Sunday school and church, as you did in those days, there was a certain element of understanding of what the Bible was on about. However, when confronted with death and his own mortality, a personal battle went on in Gordon for some time. One day in 1948, which he remembers well (including the three horses and the paddock where he was ploughing), he got down on his knees and committed his life to his Lord Jesus. Gordon says, 'Jesus Christ makes life make sense.'

That Gordon links his love of God with his hunting and time in the mountains was significant for me as we connected over the classic hunt he recalled for his part of this book: just a small memory of this wonderful man.

I'll leave it to Gordon himself to have the last word via part of a poem written in his latter years:

Almighty God, creator of the Universe, maker of Heaven and Earth.
Thank you for planet earth but thank you for our special land, deep in the Southern Ocean.
'The land of the long white cloud'.

For the mighty mountain peaks and alpine valleys
The great birch forests, the giant trees of the lowlands
For the joy we have in experiencing the wonders of these special places

For the thunder of the hanging glaciers
As thousands of tons break off and crash to the valley floor

For the mighty wapiti bull as he bugles out his challenge that echoes across the wilderness amphitheatre

[And after several similar verses:]

Thank you for the pleasures we have in camping in these 'great outdoors'
Thank you that you reveal yourself, O God, so wondrously in your creation
O that man everywhere might see and believe and turn again to our God and saviour.

The sentiments expressed for Fiordland's wild places, the wapiti and the connections Gordon had shared all resonated well with me during our talks. It was a great pleasure to have met the man.

Thank you, Gordon.

Chapter 4

South Westland throws down the challenge

Intimidating!

We were sitting in Lame Duck Hut in the Karangarua when I'd asked my two experienced hunting buddies Shaun Moloney and Jansen Travis what words they'd use to describe hunting in South Westland.

'Intimidating' seemed to sum up the discussions that followed.

It's the overall sense of challenge that goes with hunting in this region of New Zealand that makes it special. The challenges of weather and terrain can turn any hunting trip there into an adventure, at any time. As one cobber put it, the east coast region is fine 80 per cent of the time and wet for the other 20 per cent, whereas on the western side the ratios are reversed! South Westland seems to be constantly in a state of vapour — at least when I go hunting.

We'd planned a trip aiming to take advantage of such windows of east–west weather during an eight-day spell we'd each arranged away from our various work responsibilities. The aim was to hunt for big bull tahr in December and the plan was loosely based around being mobile and keeping our eye on the MetVUW weather service as the time drew near. Trying to predict weather with modern forecasting tools and rain radars has certainly come a long way but essentially can still be thwarted by Mother Nature! Our well-hatched flexibility was to be so easily undone!

As the time drew nearer there were several cellphone calls that seemed to twirl around conversation points such as the following:

'It looks like the rain prediction would give us two clear days on the Monday/Tuesday and then the weather will just dump on Wednesday.'

'Yeah, that low is showing yellow all Wednesday. That's a heap of rainfall, mate.'

'So we should hunt the east coast then ... something close, maybe up the front country of the Lawrence and then we walk out in the drizzle on Tuesday evening and drive around to the west coast through the night and walk in to Welcome Flat in the rain.'

'Man, that's a big day!'

'Yeah, but the walk in will all be on tracks — "loopie" tracks and all the main side creeks will have bridges over them, so no high creeks to get over. And there're the hot pools, too, at Welcome Flat. We could share those with blonde Swiss tourist gals!'

'But then we won't wanna get out hunting when the weather lifts ...'

'I dunno. That low could stall. What if there're fronts racked and stacked up in behind that system. We'd end up with torrential stuff chucking it down the whole week.'

'Well, it looks like it's clearing on Wednesday evening. There'll be cooler air in behind that. That'll be great, none of that West Coast fog hanging around the tops for most of the day and stuffing up the viz. And the big bulls will be out grabbing some break from the soaking they will have had.'

And so the conversation would go on and on while we watched progress of the weather systems when the forecast mapping was updated; we'd also cross-reference that with what the Met Service was predicting on their website.

But, as I said, so much for planning! This was South Westland, after all, and anything can happen when coordinating plans for hunting with the weather. I'm sure there are many hunters who know exactly the scenarios that can unfold.

The consequence of that trip was that we decided to ring James Scott, the helicopter operator on the West Coast, and get his opinion of our rough draft plan. We also made the mistake of asking if there was any chance of a 'back-load' on any work he was doing in the Karangarua. That changed everything!

James could lift us to Christmas Flat Hut on a back-load he was doing (read 'cheap flight to get into the headwaters'). Suddenly, the plan altered; the east coast option was dropped and we decided to grab the quick access to the headwaters of the Karangarua and hunt that area while the weather held. We would transfer to the mid-sections while the weather did its thing and we'd be all comfy in a hut and well placed for fly camping when the weather lifted. A pretty half-decent plan!

And so it was that we found ourselves doing a quick sort of gear at James's hangar and allowing ourselves some extra food from the stash, seeing as we weren't going to be lugging it all the way via shanks's pony. (After all, it was basically downhill from the headwaters back to the road-end, wasn't it?)

Helicopter pilot James Scott yarns while last-minute packing is sorted. *Greig Caigou*

One of the things we did decide about hunts in South Westland is that many hunters' experiences of this vast and intimidating region have in fact involved Jamie Scott and Alpine Helicopters. There is easy access to the back-country from his base below Fox Glacier township and for relatively short flights you can be airlifted right into the major catchments that lie at his back door. These flights into close country are at very reasonable rates as well and he offers such a dedicated service to hunter parties. He understands his core business from this sector and he appreciates what hunters come for and their needs. He also works hard when the weather situations are putting pressure on parties stuck in the hills and wanting out. I've experienced first-hand an amazing flight out of the upper Whataroa seemingly just a few feet above the deck as the cloud layer dropped and dropped. We negotiated downstream through tight canyons, weaving our way back to the coastline with the ribbon of raging river as our route-guide.

You have to wonder what South Westland hunts would look like for many parties without Jamie's service.

Another thing about this region is that there's such a sense of journey just to get there in the first place, let alone into where the hunting actually begins. This is much the same with Fiordland. Hunters often come together after travelling by plane, vehicle and ferry and then getting across to the coast and then on down to South Westland. Or if hunters are coming up from further south there are the big drives up and over the Haast Pass, with no real stops available for last-minute shopping for anything forgotten during the packing.

The journey to the area involves plenty of coordination, as does the sorting of gear. I often find myself arriving at the region carrying too much stuff, which invariably means some sorting out with others as we rationalize the final packing at the road-end.

It all just looks like such a huge pile of gear and yet it all has to fit into those packs — packs that we'll end up carrying! Will we take that ice axe now as the weather looks really settled and the snow has gone back a lot? If we're planning to fly camp, let's just use our bivvy bags now and leave the fly behind! (Yeah, but it'll be good if the weather turns to custard) … and do we really need that much 'back-up' food? Endless questions and decision making.

I love the sense of mission that goes with a trip into South Westland. There's all that planning and coordination that culminates at the road-head with that final sorting and trying to manage for contingencies in the wilds that lie beyond the tourist views from the highway.

And make no mistakes. There's little room for poorly equipped parties in this country. Intimidating it is and ready to deal out some harsh lessons to those who do not have experience or wits enough to be well prepared and ready to do the hard work that goes with the terrain and weather conditions.

James Scott discussing flight options with Shaun. *Greig Caigou*

Such were our considerations, too, as we set about the final touches as mission time drew near and James completed his final checks of the heli.

I'm sure many hunters can relate to the sense of adventure that elevates your excitement levels as the chopper lifts off and works away across the flats, gaining altitude as the mountains start to draw closer. Soon enough you start to cast your eye about on both sides of the capsule as subtropical rainforest drifts by below and mountainsides start to draw in beside you. Here the rainforest begins to merge with twists of rocks and ice and then you see it: the first river gorge tightens in and great boulders toss raging water from side to side as it cascades down a cataract. The Hughes 500 whines away, gaining altitude above the constriction.

The international visitors who come here to hunt easily acknowledge that this is a special place on the planet. It's a real treat to take it all in with eyes wide with wonderment as the wilderness unfolds all around.

We pass close by great cliffs and James is busy through the headset pointing out places with opportunities for tahr — as he's probably pointed those same places to other hunter groups as well!

Passing over two tiny clearings there are small mobs of tahr galloping into the scrub and all the while our eyes flitter back and forth taking in features that can look deceptively insignificant from the air. There's a lesson for those who have not taken on South Westland before. The intimidation is lurking there — just in the background, hidden behind the thrill of the

chopper ride, hidden behind the speed and ease of access —
hidden, but waiting for when it's time to get down to business!

We've been to South Westland before, but even we fall victim
and are lulled by the wonder of it all.

At Christmas Flat the chopper departs and suddenly all is
quieter and the sound of the mountains settles in around us.
Jaw-dropping scenery in every direction, haunts of mighty tahr
begging to be studied through crystal-clear optics and such
pristine weather that belies what we knew lay ahead.

Tahr hunting is all about time spent spotting. *Greig Caigou*

Having already decided that we'd adopt our old stratagem,
we turn away from the temptations to stay and hunt into the
headwaters, as many other parties would do. If that's what
others would naturally do then we'll try the opposite way. So

we donned our packs and began to make our way downstream towards Lame Duck Hut with a view to sussing out the bull tahr en route. Hopefully, we'd set ourselves up for a good hunt tomorrow; before the expected trough of poor weather hit the region.

Bull tahr. *Michael McClunie*

The route is through variable terrain and we take regular pauses at spots that offer good vantage points for glassing faces on either side of the valley. There are plenty of tahr about, but we see only nannies and small bunches of juvenile bulls. We know the big fellas will be coming out closer to dark and will be active close down, mostly in the bush and scrub. At one spot we look up into some chunky cliffs above the track on the true left and spy a bull right out on the sheer face of rock. He stands out starkly with his lighter colour and while impressive my cobber still ranks him as a 'juvie', knowing that the older bulls have still got a darker colouring, even at this time of the year.

There are other bulls up in tight little corners of this bluff and we study them for longer. There are many years of combined tahr-hunting experience among us but we still comment in awe as to whether there is any place that tahr will not go. How could you hunt such animals? This is another of the intimidating aspects of hunting in South Westland. If targeting tahr, they are often in places that defy any illusion of easy or comfortable hunting. It's very off-putting to try to figure how you'd even get up to the animals' terrain, let alone get in a shot or retrieve a fallen beast.

The scrub is super tight, with great slabs of rock protruding at all manner of acute angles. There appears few breaks in the overall system that give away details of how to get up onto the cliffs or to at least close the gap for an opportunity of a good shot.

With a click of the button on his Leica Geovid binoculars, Shaun can tell us that the closest bull is 480 metres away, which is within comfortable range of a couple of us, but we're not after these juvenile bulls and so won't be making any effort to get closer. We figure there must be a bigger fellow somewhere up there hidden in the scrub and that he'll probably appear late in the evening. The plan is to keep looking and scoping out likely spots for big bull tahr as we progress downstream looking for a good camp site.

Soon enough we decide that we've come far enough downstream that we may as well finish the last leg to the hut. We'll base ourselves there and have a late evening peep further downstream to get the full lay of the opportunities in this area. En route we decide to take an animal for camp meat should we come across one, and I happen to be at the front when we come over a rise and spy our camp meat at about 12 metres! However, the resultant missed shot has gone down in the record book of shame and I fully deserved all the mocking I got on that trip ... and have had ever since! Suffice to say, I taught that young bull a lesson about feeding on the track and one day in a few years I'd hope to have a second close encounter with him.

It's certainly true that in South Westland you need to place yourself well when poor weather threatens. Many parties carry mountain radios with them and this is good practice generally, especially if you have the luxury of a fly in, fly out trip, where the weight of a radio is less of a concern. We had not taken a radio because our plan was to travel light and fly camp as we hunted our way out of the Karangarua catchment. We did know that the weather was due to close in dramatically on Wednesday and we anticipated that our next day would be the only real hunting we'd get for a while. This is the vagary of hunting in South Westland and also why you need to think ahead about where you are camped when such weather strikes.

Prior to Lame Duck Hut there is a small stream which you climb down a couple of metres into. You cross the ankle-deep streamlet and then climb up a similar-sized bank before making the last 100 metres to the hut. By the evening of the next day this stream was overflowing its banks and gushing into the main river. This heaving brown torrent was in full flood with boulders rumbling and all manner of debris hurtling along in a maelstrom of wild forces that left no doubt that this region can throw down hardship and danger in full measure.

It can also throw down massive exhilaration, too! Lightning cracks open the heavens, thunder booms off the cliffs, and waterfalls eject great volumes of water off lofty ledges and all the while pummels you with a proper sense of your place in the midst of this wildness — and much later a sense of adventure and of achievement. It's this sense of epic that truly makes the 'Coast' what it is and draws hunters and other adventurers back again and again.

We were stranded in that hut for the next day as streams upstream and downstream rose to uncrossable levels. We ate away the time entertaining ourselves with food treats, games of checkers on the floor, idle chatter, philosophizing and taking outdoor showers in our 'birthday suits'. Much like in Fiordland, these downtimes go with the territory and yet are an integral part of hunting and, in my humble opinion, are as much of what it's all about for many of us — just as much as drawing down on the trigger for meat or a trophy.

Some hunting of sorts did resume, though, as we resolved to move further downstream once we could and to try to locate areas that bigger bulls were hiding in. We suspected they were mostly in the bush and that we would need different tactics. Of course, animals are where you find them and so you have to be there in the first place. All areas are worth a look. We all knew, for example, of an incident where two hunters had recovered 13-inch bulls from the clearing across from the hut! (Sadly, these were already dead, peppered with buckshot from aerial culling. This somewhat mocked the parameters of the tahr herd management strategy, where mature bulls are supposed to be left alive outside national parks and only nannies culled to achieve the desired animal densities.)

Lame Duck Hut sanctuary. *Greig Caigou*

So we hunted under cliff edges, right in among the thicker bush, and at times found where animals had been holed up during the worst of the weather. Later in the day we went through areas well eaten out by the animals. However, the older bulls were still eluding us and more nannies and young kids started to appear in the country where we were hoping to locate big bulls.

Shaun peers through the wet weather for tahr. *Greig Caigou*

At one spot we had some fun getting in closer to a few sets of nannies sitting off from the main mobs while they tended their young. This made for some video opportunities and some good footage presented itself and I was able to trial a new lightweight tripod while hidden in among the scrub.

Once disturbed by my filming antics, these nannies made off

and alerted a bull that must have been lying down unnoticed in the lower scrub. Shaun decided to shoot this animal as it appeared to have one gammy leg, which wasn't looking so healthy. With a bit of a scurry I was soon frantically trying to set up the tripod, extending the legs at all sorts of angles against the side of a large rock and swinging the camera around trying to locate the bull in the viewfinder. What a rush. This was more fun than lining up on the animal with a rifle!

Shaun Moloney with a storm bull. *Greig Caigou*

Finding the bull in wide view I settled in behind the camera and zoomed in — not too far as to pixelate the footage but close enough to give a good sense of the shot to come. Once sorted I gave the OK to Shaun, who all this while had been through the same sorts of motions in lying across the rock and finding the animal in the scope while settling his breathing down for accuracy. A couple of good killing shots were sent on their way at a fair range, although the bull did require a third hit to ensure it stayed down dead.

All this was some much needed mountain excitement for Shaun, who'd spent the last three months offshore in the confines of a drilling operation where he supervised dive crews working on the sea floor.

We moved on down to Cassel Flat Hut to wait out the weather clearance we so longed for and arrived there drenched and glad for the fireplace with some drying racks. This is a comfy wee hut and is surrounded by large grassy flats with many more little pockets of open ground tucked away into the bush fringes. Already on this trip we had seen over 100 tahr, some chamois and deer, and these clearings promised some venison to carry out, judging by the amount of sign.

For now, though, the plan was still to search out the big bull tahr and with the expected weather clearance on hold we hoped for a clearing sky overnight, hatching plans for an early morning stalk of the local country before heading high to a bivvy camp in the morning.

We were away before first light and sneaked off in different directions to check out the main flats but especially the little pockets around the edges of these clearings. We were very clear about one another's whereabouts and agreed a rough time to be back at the hut for breakfast.

I enjoyed the anticipation of hugging the scrub edges in the fine misty rain, ever expectant that a feeding deer would come into view as I slowly rounded each new corner. Time dragged on, though, and the light rain got heavier and so did my feelings that this trip was not going to work out.

Many of you will know that growing sense of a long-awaited trip drawing a blank and not turning out as hoped for. That's hunting, however, and in theory I knew this was a possibility when considering the vagaries of hunting in this region. I guess I had just hoped for something different this time.

My stalking for deer lost its interest and I eventually resigned myself to the inevitability of turning back and slowly settled into a sloshing plod back to the hut.

Drying out at Cassel Flat Hut. *Greig Caigou*

The mood was a little sombre back at Cassel Flat Hut. Each of us tried to talk up the possibilities of a clearance or perhaps even having another poke around in the thick scrub back upriver, but the rain just persisted and ultimately one of us made the call. Pull the pin and head out.

Once the rational decision was out there we just each took it on board and set to with packing up, cleaning out the hut and wriggling back into wet gear. Before long we were on our way again ... down the track and heading for the main road bridge.

A minor mocking of the cloud layer teased us with a patch of clearer sky, but within a few minutes that too closed in again and the rain thrashed down some more.

There are three side streams of consequence between Cassel Flat and the main road and when we came to the first of them we were greeted by quite high water and a fairly quick flow. I eyed up and down the toss and ebbs of the flow and strode in at what appeared the best place. That quickly revealed itself to be a solid flow and I eased up, taking care and making sure of my footing. I turned around and reached out for Jansen's faithful walking pole and with that extra 'leg' was able to get some stronger purchase on the bottom and gain the other bank. Shaun followed and mid-stream relayed 'Mr Stick' back to Jansen for his crossing.

The second stream held even more flow, but those who know this area will be familiar with the big log that is firmly wedged above the main stream and a good crossing can be made here. Of course, this is nothing like those 'challenge ropes courses' they have at outdoor education centres. Firm pole, rushing water underneath but no rope belay!

We could have used our short section of rope but all of us were experienced, with confidence in our footing. We were able to make a judgment call and bypass some health and safety risk management procedure. Some have been foolhardy around rivers, though, and even experienced mountain people have met their demise in New Zealand's back-country rivers. Skill and confidence develop over time from just being out there in the hills and taking on more and more extending situations. South Westland is good for building that kind of experience and judgment.

However, the next and final stream crossing challenged that confidence and judgment greatly.

We came through the bush to an increasingly ominous sound ahead of us and upon reaching the edge of the terrace above the crossing looked down to a foaming torrent that rushed towards the fully raging main river just 100 metres away. This was another matter altogether, and we stood and studied the lie of the land with a bit more focused attention now!

We checked around for the best crossing. Initially, we worked our way downstream to see if the water might fan out more before surging into the main river, but this was not the case. A long way upstream we could see some possibilities, but the river wasn't waiting and we knew the level was rising quickly with the deluge that was coming down in the headwaters.

Now this is a matter for serious consideration because many an outdoors person knows that the last crossing before safety is the most dangerous one. 'Get-home-itis' is perilous, and no call from the outside world is worth attempting a dangerous river crossing. I recall reading somewhere that even that most experienced West Coast explorer, Charlie Douglas, had noted that being unable to swim had saved his life many times!

We felt we could do it, though, and with two walking poles grasped between the three of us we moved forward into an area where the foaming bubbles stalled somewhat in their pandemonious rush and surge towards the brown mass of the main Karangarua River.

Moving forward with constant communication between us we first set firm a person who had the best, solid footing. Then the others used that as an anchor to move forward and keep the line braced in the current. At times it was me as anchor in the downstream position, where the water was shallowest but gaining momentum as it cascaded over the lip of the rocks into the next reach. At other times it was Jansen in the upstream and deeper water, up to his waist and pressured with white, aerated water.

But soon we had fought our passage across and we all felt that wee surge of adrenaline easing as we shook ourselves off, laughing about who got their balls the wettest and gabbling as the body soaked in the extra strength of an obstacle overcome.

The rest of the journey out was uneventful and only required that solid grind of nose down and feet moving forward as we strode along through flooded bush tracks and boulder hopped along riverbeds. My shoulders ached somewhat and the pack required frequent shrugs both left and right or up and down on the waist belt in order to alleviate the minor pains of 'swagging'. At these times it's all about attitude. You can be sore, wet and miserable *or* you can be just sore and wet!

Eventually, though, we made the final flats with the main road bridge in sight. Before long I managed to wave down a car at the bridge and hitch a ride back up to our vehicle at James Scott's shed. In no time we were out of our soaking gear, out of the hills and on our ways again.

That's another sojourn in South Westland completed.

Travelling up the highway towards home a few days later and reflecting on the trip, with the benefit of hindsight I came to appreciate that I would have been better to stay in one place and sneak around in the rain, bush hunting the canyon sides and thick scrub where the bigger bulls must have been spending their days.

To some extent I had known this anyway, but something in me didn't want to hunt tahr this way!

I was struggling with some sort of puritan image of tahr on cliff faces, manes fanned in the wind, seemingly impervious to the rain, the cliffs and, in fact, superior to everything in their environment. This is how I like to see tahr in South Westland. It fits my personal vision of this amazing animal and this region.

The reality, though, is that these animals need to live; they know where the food is and the needs of their bodies through differing seasons and they know, too, where their best options for survival are as the gunships of the sky beat and twirl among the ramparts they call home.

I need to adapt better to these patterns and changes in the habits of these wild animals, just as much as I need to adapt my somewhat inflexible plans to the environment and weather

113

vagaries of this region. I was reminded that I needed to relearn what I already knew about hunting in South Westland and to be less fixated upon my preferred hunting style. I needed to adjust my timings and expectations, and regain that connectedness to the ways of the animals and their wild environment.

This trip didn't rate as a success in some hunters' terms.

There were no red-letter days. There were no trophy animals shot. There are no photos of big bulls, no magazine stories to tell. Not even any meat brought home!

Yes, I was disappointed in not achieving the goal I'd set. But the trip did rate for me in the end. It was a refreshing reminder of what I love about hunting in New Zealand — and particularly in South Westland.

Some go to the mountains to pit themselves against nature, the animals or to match themselves against others. There are those only interested in achieving some quest (such as a trophy moment or gathering a physical representation of that moment — or indeed a trophy). Still others use mountaineering, hunting or fishing as an excuse for 'getting away from it all' in isolated places.

You can also go into the mountains and wilderness to help raise your awareness of and responsiveness to natural surroundings. The aim is not thrill seeking or a search for a bigger ego perhaps, but rather for greater personal mastery.

Being able to live and move around safely, at ease with the intimidation factor that is South Westland, requires much more than just skill at walking or navigation; it requires knowledge that can only be got over time by being there, in the mountains and learning to read and respond to signs within yourself.

This is self-knowledge as well as knowledge of the wilderness environment, and the two eventually come together as a sense of belonging, of feeling at home there.

For me, it's a bit of this! A bit of a running towards these things that wild places foster in me rather than a running away from the workaday world. I love it when my busy life is reset to a wilder rhythm — at a similar pace to nature. When I'm engaging with the harshness of South Westland, as a hunter, I sense more strongly that connectedness with nature, her wilderness ways, the animals and in fact all wildlife.

Of course, what we get out of our hunting trips depends to a large extent on what we seek in the first place. Being aware that it's not always about downing an animal is a bit of a revelation for some.

Knowing what you actually want from the hunting ultimately shapes *how* you hunt.

Unfortunately, I didn't see it clearly enough at the time of this trip into South Westland. I think I was too focused on the wrong objectives. It's not about the bull tahr — mostly! At times I just value being out there in wild places, in all of that drama of the wild weather we had on this trip. I loved being part of the deluge. I loved the spike of adrenaline getting across that wee torrent on the walk out. While it was not too difficult, I still loved getting out to the main road and feeling like I'd gotten out, survived on nature's terms and with our own good judgments, when other parties elsewhere at the time were being 'rescued' and flown out of the back-country because of horrendous weather and high rivers.

I loved sitting in the comforts of a café in Fox Glacier having

115

a coffee en route home as well. I'd had my shot of the back-country and was ready to return to the other, workaday, world.

I loved the fullness of yet more experience in this rugged region. I was feeling more at home in this truly wild country and this was all part of a more real way of living, for me.

Thanks, South Westland!

For me, this is the curious allure of the region. Daunting and intimidating it is, but that is what makes it really special. We return from those hills with a bigger sense of our ability to cope, more so than we do from our hunts in the easier country. We've proven ourselves — at least to ourselves (and that is important). There's an enlargement of spirit; we've accomplished something ... inside, at least.

Like Fiordland, South Westland draws you back too — for more!

Chapter 5

Zeff Veronese — a hunter in paradise

'The Douglas hunt was our first hunt into the big country of the West Coast. That place has magic! It's tough, it's beautiful — it has everything!

'I still recall seeing 200-plus animals of all three species jostling for position as they made their getaway along the same trail. There were big bull tahr, nannies, chamois and red deer charging and cutting in on each other as they galloped around the slope, fleeing toward a well-known escape route.

'I flew back in there at the start of 2010 with three old-time friends, one from Italy, and the excitement of that first trip still rose up in me as we zipped along in the chopper over country through which we'd humped our packs. That first exploration set me up for many, many years of hunting trips all over those Southern Alps: the Karangarua, Whataroa, Whanganui, Landsborough, the Godley, Rakaia and so many more. I love it.'

For Zeff Veronese, hunting had always been in his blood, right from when he was a boy in Italy chasing snakes, rats, birds, moles, frogs; whatever he could hunt. This continued during the years he lived in Christchurch, hopping on his bike to get out to McLeans Island to shoot rabbits, hares, ducks and quail. With his mum being such a great cook she was able to turn anything into a great meal and the immigrant Veronese family didn't buy any meat for over nine years, living completely off what the boys would procure with their hunting skills.

But it was in December 1964 that this classic hunting memory began for Zeff as he and his brother Ennio took off on their annual holiday trip with a whirlwind driving tour checking out the scenery at the bottom of the South Island. This was all new country for them and the FJ Holden took on everything, including a confrontation with a tourist bus inside the Homer Tunnel, which most folk know is a one-way passage controlled by signal lights — a point the boys hadn't noted!

Returning via the West Coast and arriving at Fox Glacier they had hoped to do some shooting and were taken aback when the Forest Service ranger informed them all the blocks had been booked up for months. A stroke of fate followed when the ranger mentioned that one small party of two had wanted to do an airdrop of food into the Douglas Valley but had been delayed for a week because of bad weather. When the ranger said that the Douglas was tough country but that there was plenty of room for more hunters, Zeff and Ennio set off in search of the men with some hope that they might link up with that party.

In good fashion the hunters obliged and the boys joined them in wrapping up a food drop. First each item of food was wrapped with paper then put inside a sugar bag, which in turn went into a larger wheat bag and then was packed all around with straw. This bag was compressed and sewn closed.

Dave from the other party departed with the pilot and got the job of free-dropping the bags from what was a very low height as the plane slowed to almost stalling speed over some flats in the upper valley. When Dave returned with tales of mobs of tahr everywhere the excitement was already beginning to mount, even though he'd also reported the country was pretty steep-looking.

I remember those same thoughts when I first flew into Horace Walker Hut in mid-winter with Goodwin McNutt in the mid-1970s. It was daunting to a young 17 year old and the walk out looked even more formidable!

That route was what Zeff, his brother and the other party used for their trip, taking six hours to get up the Karangarua to the wire crossing and then on up into the Regina.

I'll let Zeff pick up the story from here:

This section proved to be quite challenging as the track often led you into a bluff and you then had to go looking for where it restarted. We eventually reached the crossing over the Regina and it carried a fair bit of clear water.

Ennio was first to cross the two-wire cable and when he was nearing the middle of the crossing, the wires proved quite loose and they twisted around so that Ennio found himself in the horizontal position looking straight down into the torrent. And all this with a pack load on. That settled the matter for all of us and once Ennio managed to extricate himself we all got down onto the riverbank and opted for a more controlled crossing of the river, rather than a dunking!

The exertions of the day meant we ran out of light and spent the night camped partway up the steep haul that takes you up onto Conical Hill saddle.

Crossing the Karangarua en route to the Douglas Valley. *Zeff Veronese*

The next day saw us cresting the final pitch and we had the first view of the mighty Douglas Valley. It was impressive and I was sure excited by what might lie ahead.

We'd been told that there were two routes into the headwaters, one along through the alpine tops and the other from the bottom of the valley. Neither looked too good but we decided on the latter on the basis that if the weather closed in we could be better sheltered in the bush.

Before descending into the bush we spotted a mob of about 10 chamois some 300 yards away, which was a good omen.

The valley floor route proved to be as tough as it looked and a very trying experience. (Anyone who has been in this country will know the rather daunting struggle of the terrain and for a first-timer in South Westland it would either set you up for further adventuring and pitting yourself against the tests of such wilderness or, instead, put you right off such places because of the sheer hardness required by stalkers to access the hunting country.)

Sometimes it took as much as half an hour to cover 100 yards and at times we could peer down into great intimidating slots in the canyon, but we just had to slug it out. By the evening we finally came into a small clearing and set up camp. Tired as we were we made a good job of that camp, setting up a stone fireplace as was our usual custom and getting everything well prepared so we would be free to hunt.

Dave and Brian hadn't brought much food with them so of course we shared, but that was going to put a strain on our own supplies over the remaining days so Ennio climbed a nearby tree in the hope of spotting some handy meat to add to the rations.

Now Ennio and I always carried a slingshot, which was a legacy from our days back in Italy as young boys. We could hit anything with those weapons. Ennio fired a stone down to near me and we thought he must have missed the bird or whatever he was trying to bag. Soon enough another stone landed and with the mental telepathy of brothers-in-arms I knew that he was signalling me and as soon as I'd grabbed my .30-06 and jumped in his direction a chamois ran out in front of me. I had so little time to react that I shot it from the hip at 15 yards.

With polythene and other materials Zeff turned a rock shelter into a good camp site.
Zeff Veronese

Of course we had a fresh meal of sliced backsteaks, which were a bit chewy but still delicious, and with full bellies, a warm camp and the great valley all around we knew we were in for a wonderful trip.

The next day we looked across the Douglas River to the flat clearing that is opposite where Horace Walker Hut is now.

There was that large mob of about 200 animals — deer, tahr and chamois — and I'll never forget them all running for the only escape route up the hill at the end of that clearing. With so many animals jostling for position it was chaotic and we just watched and laughed so hard we never fired a shot at them.

We chose to hunt up the valley that day and as our airdrop had been into the top basin of the Douglas we carried on towards it. All the while we looked up the mountainsides on the Horace Walker glacier and we could see mobs of 40 to 50 animals on every clearer patch of ground and this was at any time of the day. Almost every side creek we crossed had some chamois or tahr not much higher than the riverbed.

We crossed the Douglas moraine above the lake and for a while we travelled on the true left. When we were far enough to get into the top basin and seeing no options we decided to climb the last 15 yards up the very steep moraine wall to get into the top basin. Now a fall here would have meant falling under the ice that had melted against the rock sides. There was this slot between the rock and the ice and about 20 yards down underneath we could hear the river. This was not a pleasant thought as we scrambled precariously up the sides, and just a short distance from the top it became too steep to negotiate and all four of us were holding on for our lives! Ennio was nearest the top and with great courage slowly made it up. A length of rope was produced and one by one we got pulled up. From that day on I've always made it even more of a point to carry a length of rope into these mountains.

Not too far distant was the Harpers Rock Bivvy and we made that our home for the remainder of our hunting time and started looking for our food sacks. We found them, but a lot of the contents were damaged with the fall and some sugar mixed with salt and other such injustices greeted us! As a whole, though, we were thankful for the extra rations and most food was salvaged.

The Douglas Glacier from the head of the top basin. *Zeff Veronese*

Once we were set up and relaxed we finally looked around and took stock of our position. We couldn't help but marvel at the majestic beauty of the Douglas Glacier with the thick slabs of snow ready to break off with a sound like thunder. All around us the mountains were steep but beautiful and not too far above the glacier névé Mt Sefton was visible if we climbed a little.

Tahr were everywhere we looked!

A mob of about 40 nannies and kids were feeding 300

yards away level with the rock bivvy and in this same area one morning I shot two chamois with one bullet. This was not intentional but the numbers of game present meant that this was a very real possibility at times.

Ennio and I went hunting into the head of the basin and climbed up Douglas Pass that separates the McKerrow Glacier, from which the mighty Landsborough River is born. Right on the Pass we couldn't believe it when we saw an eight-point stag and two hinds. They started climbing up the steep ridge and we wondered how far they would climb and so followed them. At one point when they were perhaps 50 yards ahead they got bluffed and we could see the stag's antlers moving around excitedly behind a rock. He knew we were there and the stag had a look and we could see his face. When he saw that we were still coming he came out into the open. He first looked at us and then at the steep McKerrow Glacier below. Then he took another look at us and again at the glacier; he was boxed in and this was his escape route. All of a sudden he placed his front hooves out onto the ice of the glacier and with his front legs stiff he just launched off and skied on down. After about 100 yards the slope eased and he started running. The hinds followed on and they soon disappeared in the distance. Amazing!

We carried on climbing until we reached the highest point. The rocks were mainly big slabs and they just seemed to rest on one another. We could stand on them and look down onto McKerrow Glacier. At one point, on looking around we realized the rock we were standing on was suspended out in mid-air and all was empty below us. We made a quick getaway!

Later, on our descent, we were on some hard snow and could

see down below there was a beautiful shallow basin and we conceived the idea of sliding down the slope on our bums with our Japara parkas under us. In a short distance we started gaining velocity at an alarming rate and when I spotted a thin black thing protruding from the ice ahead of me I went into a panic, jumping my legs in front of me to try to alter course.

I barely made it and we ended up safely below, but the thought of my virility being shattered on that sharp rock made me much more careful in future.

Dave and Brian hunted in their own directions, but the next day we hunted up-valley hoping to get onto a mob of six mature bulls again as we'd been foiled in our stalking attempts because of some noisy keas. This time, after a good stalk we secured some of these bulls and during our descent we observed four trampers coming down the Douglas Pass. We knew that to be so far away from civilization it would have taken these trampers several days of eating dehydrated peas, carrots and spuds without any fresh meat so we took it upon ourselves to supply them with some.

In a small valley between them and us we spotted some chamois so we shot one and the trampers started yelling and making noises in case we shot at them. We yelled back that we had seen them and quickly made our way over to the chamois and took off the choicest bits of meat. Not long later we met them and asked if they wanted some meat and they all happily agreed. While walking with them towards the bivvy, I spotted one tahr nearly 1000 yards above us on an overhanging rock that looked like a matchstick. For some reason, and maybe a bit of bravado, I decided to shoot at it from where we all were.

126

I had a Pecar 4x scope with a post and two side posts so I settled the main post on the top of this matchstick rock formation, which was a nice straight up and down line, and then I aimed about 20 feet above the animal. The first shot made a small dust hit about 20 feet below the tahr so next shot I doubled my distance above the animal and what seemed a whole second in time later the nanny fell over, freefalling 300 yards before she connected with the rock wall in a great cloud of flying fur. Of course, the audience was surprised and praised me for my marksmanship (but I'm sure it had been the biggest fluke that has ever happened to me!).

Bull tahr (12.5 inches), a favourite game animal for Zeff. *Zeff Veronese*

That night while we hunters were trying to sleep at the bivvy, the starved trampers were up cooking meat until midnight!

We had not really got onto any good trophy-sized bulls up in the headwaters so we decided to pack up and work our way down to the Horace Walker area again. Ennio and I hunted up behind the camp and we spotted a mob of about 20 bulls. Ennio drew the long straw and selected his bull. After his shot all hell broke loose.

Above us was a sheer face and all the animals charged down towards us. I hit one on the run just 30 yards away, and with the momentum the poor animal just didn't stop and I had to give him another shot at point blank range. The bull cascaded on and Ennio was on a little ledge some 10 yards below and I yelled 'Look out!' as the thrashing bull fell just where Ennio had been half a second before. There was a bit of silence between us — it took a little while for the colour to return to his face — but as soon as it did we both cracked up, laughing out loud. Of course, we couldn't hit any more tahr after that, even though they all were still charging down the sheer slope all around us.

Later that day we split up to cover more country and a while later I spotted a mature bull at 300 yards near the bottom of the mountain. Soon after shooting that bull a red stag in velvet passed by only 150 yards away, but I let him go because I was eager to get over to the downed bull. Soon after that a chamois poked his head up and as he looked shootable I shot him also. After quickly sawing off the skullcap and horns, which were of good length, I continued my descent only to come upon a hind and fawn lower down. In those days slinkies and fawn skins were used for making women's handbags so I shot the fawn as well and it was then that I realized I had shot all three species of animals in not much more than five minutes.

The bull turned out to be a very solid 12¾ inches.

What a time we were having! Animals were everywhere and every new gully we moved into presented new opportunities and action. Ennio and I both had to crawl right through the middle of big mobs of tahr on two separate occasions to get to our chosen bulls. In those days we wore khaki-coloured overalls to camouflage ourselves against the tussock and at one stage I recall being only one yard away from a feeding nanny as I crawled closer and closer to my bull. If one stopped feeding to look at me, I would freeze for a few seconds and the animals would just resume feeding. In this way I made it through the mob without flushing the animals and the poor bull beyond would suffer the consequences. It was exciting stuff being in that country at close quarters with the animals and possibly in those days the animals hadn't learned just how dangerous the human species could be.

Another time, there was a mob of about 30 bulls and I was on top of them. While I was trying to work out which had the biggest curve, the fog rolled in and blotted out the whole scene. Well, I waited and waited for ages and in the end I packed up my gear and decided to just walk on down into the area where they were and shoot them as I got to them. I got two 12½-inch beauties just shooting from the hip!

After a few days Dave and Brian departed for the road-end as their time was up and we continued for one more day's hunt in all the likely spots nearby our camp. We crossed the river not far from the ice melt and climbed up into the bluffs. At one point while climbing up a scrubby ridge I saw a bull lying in a small depression not three yards in front of me and when he stood up I was able to shoot him from the hip. He was a very old bull, but unfortunately the horns had been badly broomed back so was still not the trophy I was after. Further up Ennio spied a similarly old bull with big body size, but he too had only a 12½-inch head, even though we aged him at over 13 years old. We did shoot another four bulls that day with one going just under 13 inches and it was one of the greatest days out after bull tahr that I experienced. We shot 55 animals on this trip, mainly bulls, but we were pretty much culling in there, as the animals were everywhere and the grasslands were getting eaten out.

Next day we decamped early in the morning and made tracks for home, each carrying six sawn-down tahr heads from the greatest valley in South Westland! It was an epic journey out as we were fit by now and set a target to make the road-end as soon as possible because we were due back at work in two days. With a heavy load and retracing our route downstream and up onto Conical Hill, we made it out to the main road bridge by nightfall, covering at least 25 kilometres in one day. We were that done in we couldn't even sleep properly!

We'd had an amazing time in that valley and the images of all those bull tahr drew me back to this and other valleys for many years after. I even took my newlywed wife, Gwen, on a walk to the very top of the Karangarua Valley, and that was no mean feat.

[I reckon that's not your common honeymoon outing either, but when I mentioned that to Zeff he argued what could be better than combining the two best loves of his life into one trip!]

The attraction, though, was not just the glorious numbers of animals we saw but the grandeur. We'd climb everywhere and we'd just climb to see what was on the other side, or go to the top of a peak just to say we'd been there. It was all this rugged and tough stuff that I loved.

What struck me about Zeff Veronese as he recounted this story from the Douglas trip is that the man is so passionate about his hunting and he still loves the high mountains for chamois and tahr hunting. In fact, he has hunted tahr most years since 1963 and had to wait 45 years until his seventieth year before he shot his 14-inch bull with a Douglas score of 45.5 — the 'tahr of a lifetime'. He has also shot seven chamois heads over 10 inches with one having a Douglas score of 29.

In 2010 when I was writing this book Zeff was 72 years 'young' and in the first half of the year had already undertaken trips for two weeks into the Catseye block during the wapiti ballot (which being in the first period struck atrocious weather) and also trips to the Jacobs, the Douglas again as well as Glentanner, Lewis Pass and Thirteen Mile Bush. In fact he puts in more days hunting on the hill than many modern-day and younger hunters log over several years!

He freely admits that his body doesn't bounce back like it used to, especially now that he recalls the very heavy loads he and his brother used to lug around the hills and especially over the distances and terrain they explored. However, he is a walking testimony and evangelist for the powers of glucosamine, which he considers a 'wonder drug' for his joints, especially his knees. Zeff recalls coming down off a high slope in the Troyte Valley several years ago (in his late sixties when most others have hung up their boots) and feeling really jaded from the jarring of the weight of his 70-pound pack! On the advice of some acquaintances he asked about some relief for the joints and got into dosing up on glucosamine and fish oil tablets.

Zeff's 14⅛-inch bull shot in very steep country just before his seventieth birthday. *Zeff Veronese*

Watching him now and listening to his exploits on the high hills it is impressive how well his body has responded to the medication, and Zeff freely and enthusiastically recounts how he feels much younger and 'full of beans'. This renewed energy and passion for the high hills shows no signs of abating, not from his health's point of view anyway, and certainly he and Gwen have figured out their relationship somewhat to tolerate his many adventures while he still can.

When he emigrated from Italy he had no idea that this pathway would so capture his affection. He tells me, though, that he always knew he loved hunting and he never in his wildest, grandest dreams would have expected that the move to New Zealand would provide all the opportunities that make his life feel as if he has been in paradise ever since.

Zeff reckons he started hunting as soon as he was around six years old — it was in his blood; in fact his father was a hunter as too was his grandfather, who had died at 91 after setting out hunting on foot in heavy snow to go after a hare. (He'd got the hare but had got a sweat up while out in the cold air and died of pneumonia three days afterwards.)

Zeff grew up in Northern Italy in the small village of Torviscosa, near Trieste, close to the border with Yugoslavia. When he was a boy he'd seen fighter planes and bombers overhead because the town had a cellulose factory, which is a native ingredient of gunpowder (and who knows, perhaps that set him on the pathway to owning firearms!).

His parents had come to that village from the Venetian province, which had been under Austrian rule until the First World War. The local kids' parents wouldn't let them play with the Veronese boys as the Austrians had fought against the Italians in the war. As a consequence the boys were picked on to some extent and they had learnt to fight from a young age. The Veronese brothers, particularly Ennio, had built up real reputations as 'toughies'.

Right from when young they'd wanted to hunt and display their trophies. The boys would kill snakes and come walking into town with these trophies hanging from a stick. If they shot different birds they'd take off their tails and nail them to a door as a trophy board, with a little note of what species it was. They shot 36 sparrows once and lined them up for display before roasting them for food. The brothers were hunters. They would catch frogs and trap fish for food and they shot plenty of rats for sport. They'd use any weapon they could lay their hands on, ranging from air rifles, bow and arrow, to blow tubes and slingshots. (In fact, Zeff treated his slingshot as a side-arm and right from his earliest years his mother had to make him a special bigger pocket in his trousers for the slingshot and his supply of small stones for ammunition.)

As we sat in the dining room chatting I had come to fully appreciate the foundations of the hunter's life that had begun all those years ago for Zeff and his brothers. They did the things of boys: running around exploring, scheming up adventures and wild antics. In dreaming up new ways to catch or kill anything that seemed to move, their 'sport' had honed their skills and created an outlandish and passionate wanderlust for seeking out game animals and new exploits. It was this passion which they brought into their adopted country.

When their sister married a New Zealand soldier she met during the war, she wrote back home saying how great the country was compared to Italy. Italy was fully broken in those days and so two of the brothers took up the challenge to come over for work in 1953. With such a strong work ethic and a land brimming with opportunity it wasn't long before Mum, Dad, three further brothers and two sisters immigrated to New Zealand as well. It was 1956 and Zeff was 18 at the time.

To support the family the boys worked various jobs and later in 1966 the four brothers bought an iron business on Lincoln Road in Christchurch. Two years later they moved and built a small factory on Blenheim Road where the Veronese Bothers wrought iron works became well known and remained at this location until they sold the business decades later in 2000.

Shotgun over shoulder, Zeff and dog head off hunting from his new home in New Zealand.
Zeff Veronese

135

The hunting back in those earliest days was all around Canterbury, and Zeff and his brothers began hunting in earnest for big game later in 1956, the year I was born. They bought a pig dog for a week's wages on condition that the guy would teach them how to hunt. They went out and managed eight pigs with this man's help, but Zeff's first pig on his own took him 35 shots before he managed a good hit with his old Mark III .303. He had more luck with his first deer, which he shot in 1958, only taking 11 shots while he was still getting the feel of his gun!

Meat from a weekend hunt. (L to R) Nephew Claudio, Zeff and brother Nadillo. *Zeff Veronese*

Nowadays there is no such lack in Zeff's skill behind the business end of a rifle, and he is a keen reloader and experimenter with all things that involve killing power. In fact,

Zeff is an ardent fan of long-barrelled rifles and cartridges loaded for supercharged velocities.

And he is opinionated on bullet type, too! Zeff doesn't subscribe to the theory that a projectile should leave all the energy in the animal. He wants it to go through and leave a good exit wound hole to bleed in case it's not an outright kill. He uses bonded bullets and Zeff found on earlier experimentation when pushing velocity with a 7 mm that a 140-grain projectile would hit a tahr and it would still go for 10 yards or so before going down. On the other hand, when he moved to 160-grain projectiles the animal would poleaxe on the spot.

'This is what you want — always go for the heaviest bullet you can push along.'

His current beast for all big game hunting is a .30-378 Weatherby that has a 32-inch barrel and fires 180-grain projectiles with 'warmish' loads at a whopping 3600 fps. One mean 'mutha load' at the dead end of such firepower! (Of course, it's just as hard hitting at the other end, too.)

Gunnery is important, however.

'You can walk for bloody miles but at the end of the day you've got to have a properly tuned rifle and know how to use it. I don't care how they look either; I want them to shoot.'

In those early years of hunting around Canterbury the other gear the boys used was largely handmade by themselves or their mum. She sewed canvas covers for their rifles, and as they had their own ducks and chickens she even sewed up a linen bag and crammed in their down feathers to make their first sleeping bags, which weighed in at around nine pounds (4 kg).

137

Zeff with an earlier version of the 'beast' — 300 Weatherby with 30-inch barrel. *Zeff Veronese*

They crafted their own packs with leather straps and welded together a frame from tubing in which they could carry cooking fuel for their little Primus cooker. The pack was very large and they carried some big loads. (Evidently, 120-pound loads were common in those days and so I'm thankful for the modern lightweight gear we get to use nowadays.)

In the early years they used clear polythene then a Japara fly and later moved to an A-frame tent with no sewn-in floor. This sort of home-grown approach has continued right up until today where Zeff is not happy to buy an off-the-shelf product for hunters, preferring instead to have a canvas maker sew up a tent fly to his own specifications. All sorts of refinements exist on his latest hunting fly, and these touches have been born out of hard-won experiences in the field.

Food for his hunting trips in those early years was typically dehydrated pea and carrot mixes and he always carried onion to supplement any meat shot on the hill. They would always eat liver first and would hang the other meat and use pepper to keep the flies off the damp joints so it would keep over a number of days. Often they'd make a stew that could then be eaten in the morning.

Zeff lugging out yet another hefty load. *Zeff Veronese*

Zeff and Ennio had bought some crampons especially for their first trip into the head of the Rangitata in 1963. Even though he'd never used them they thought it would be best to have them along on the trip into the Douglas. (They figured they could work out how best to use them once in the country!) This gear was got largely because they didn't know what to expect, but now after a lifetime of hunting such country Zeff doesn't use crampons and instead relies completely on his ice axe, which is an essential piece of gear for tahr and chamois hunting in his opinion. If the country is so severe that crampons might be required, Zeff just doesn't go there. Everywhere else the ice axe provides firm support along with the advantage of being able to cut steps and, if all else goes wrong, it can be used to self-arrest a sliding fall. He has carried in-step crampons, which have proved useful for retrieving shot animals on just a couple of occasions, but otherwise the ice axe has proved all that is necessary for most things.

Tahr hunting camp at 6000 feet. *Zeff Veronese*

On his second trip into the Douglas the brothers went in via the top route from Conical Hill and Zeff took a really big slide on some fine grass. He ended up in mortal danger as he accelerated down the slope desperately trying to regain footing. Fortunately, he made a final lunge when coming up to a tahr track that would give him some footing. So the only refinements made in gear since those earliest trips into the Douglas have been the addition of the ice axe and using good stiff, three-quarter shank boots. Of course, nowadays Zeff carries other equipment such as polar fleece layers, Gore-Tex parka, rangefinder and the like, but the basics of axe and boots ensure the fundamental safety of your footing.

'As soon as the edge of the boot is "rounded", throw the boots out of your hunting gear. For tahr hunting you never joke with your boots.'

Zeff has survived many trips now, so experience and good judgment count a considerable amount towards safe passage anyway.

As all the boys set about building their new life in Canterbury, starting a business and raising family, they progressed in their hunting endeavours as well. In 1958, almost from the very beginning, Zeff got involved with the North Canterbury Branch of the NZDA, becoming an active member right up until this day, as well as serving as Branch President for four years. After holding membership for 50 years he was made a life member.

In fact, it was on one long weekend hunt organized by the NZDA into the mighty Wilberforce Valley where I first stood alongside the North Canterbury Branch ex-army quad vehicle among the hunting 'legends' that were the Veronese brothers. As a young teenager keen on hunting I'd attended branch club nights and had marvelled at movie footage taken by Zeff Veronese. I particularly recall footage of 11 good solid stags in a mob, all in velvet, taken in the Rangitata catchments and all marching in a line right out in the tussock country. In those days I'd have been real happy to have seen just one of those animals and this only served to whet my appetite for getting out with the trainee section that the North Canterbury Branch ran for aspiring hunters.

Circa 1975 in the Wilberforce. I'm the young and keen newbie beside the quad. Zeff is on the back deck. *Greig Caigou*

You can imagine the treat it was for me then to visit Zeff at his home all these years later, meet his lovely wife, Gwen, and go out to the hunters' den in the garage. There were old sets of horns lining the garage from top to bottom. There were rows of tahr and chamois horns much like you might see atop a hunters' chalet in Europe. There were fallow racks, goat horns, pig tusks and stag antlers, and among his hunting gear was reel upon reel of movie footage shot over years on the hill.

On that first trip into the Douglas Zeff wishes he'd taken his camera because there were just so many opportunities to capture shots of animals among amazing vistas. That is why on subsequent trips Zeff got into the habit of always carrying his camera, particularly a movie camera. He has some great footage from exploits all over the country, covering off deer hunting in Dusky Sound in 1964 right through to alpine hunts as well as varied shooting forays on wallaby and hares. Zeff has taken the National NZDA trophy for film and video footage many more times than any other hunter. In 2010 it was a great honour for me to win this trophy and get my name alongside his. (Actually, I've laid down the challenge for future years and the competition is all on! It would be another treat for me to win the Zeff Veronese trophy for scenic photography at some date in the future also.) This love of photography and hunting has given Zeff a unique eye for what makes a good story on film and his footage always has some good close-up footage of animals in the wild as well.

At his garage I just wanted to shut myself in with the projector and zone out on all the scenes played out from a lifetime in the hills.

When I asked Zeff to recount a favourite or classic hunt from this vast treasure trove of memories it was moving for me to

143

have him immediately choose that hunt in the great valley of the Douglas — the very place where as a 17 year old I had first blown my perspective into a macro view and set out on my own path of discovering the hunting Meccas that lay beyond the road-ends all along the Southern Alps.

I hope another generation captures that same spark of a 'wow' trip and gets out among it to see game animals in the wild and marvel at the rich heritage and overflowing opportunities we have as hunters in this country.

The Douglas River shoot had fed his mind with things of 'paradise' and, at 72, an energized Zeff feels he doesn't have enough lifetime to do all that he'd still like to do.

I asked him what he'd say to the next generation of New Zealanders.

'Get out and do it,' was his instant reply.

'So you think it's a hunter's paradise here?'

'Yeah, bloody oath!'

Fiordland beckons. Greig Caigou

Murray Elwood glasses the head basin. Greig Caigou

Murray's first Fiordland bull. Greig Caigou

Dusk at Blue Lake in the headwaters of Wapiti River. Greig Caigou

Early morning lookout in the headwall of the Henderson Burn. Greig Caigou

Gordon Max shoots his first Fiordland wapiti in 1956. (They were asked to cull poorer beasts.) Gordon Max

Gordon Max at Stonehurst farm — Max's Bush. *Nelson Mail*

Shaun Moloney climbs into tahr country. Greig Caigou

Jansen Travis gets some water. Plenty came out of the sky later. Greig Caigou

Refuge from the storm at Lame Duck Hut. Greig Caigou

The billy fills in 23 seconds as the storm sets in! Greig Caigou

A young chamois — our premier alpine game animal. Matt Winter

Shaun and Jansen join forces crossing a South Westland side stream. Greig Caigou

Zeff Veronese, 72 years young — still hunting the tough stuff. Robbie Peck

Zeff reckoned he carried some big loads in his younger days, 100 pounds plus.
Zeff Veronese

Last day in the Douglas River, 1964. Bull tahr just under 13 inches. Zeff Veronese

Zeff regularly gets back to revisit South Westland — a hunter's paradise.
Zeff Veronese

Jansen Travis was hunting hard from a young age.
Jansen Travis

Jansen Travis with his first bull tahr. Jansen Travis

Jansen with a good wild stag from the Canterbury high country. Jansen Travis

Simon Buschl with a Nelson Lakes chamois buck. Simon Buschl

Scoped chamois in the country where Simon's story is told. Simon Buschl

Simon got up close to this velvet stag on the Nelson tops. Simon Buschl

Jessica McLees and her dad, Mike, with her first deer shot at age 13. Mike McLees

Jessica at home on Dunluce Station in Western Southland. Mike McLees

Unpacking the hunt — time in the mountains. Emma Caigou

Shaun looks over hunters' heartland in South Westland. Greig Caigou

A key motivation — seeing game animals in the wild. Matt Winter

Wilderness matters — pure delight! Greig and Emma Caigou

A memorable moment as a skilled hunter-photographer stalks a wild stag. Matt Winter

Unpacking the hunt — good mates share a warm brew. Greig Caigou

Time to pause and soak it all in. I'm blessed in the Whitcombe country. Greig Caigou

Chapter 6

Canterbury tahr hunt

It was late afternoon when I pulled the car into the lay-by and drove right in under the trees. Uncurling from the car, I eased out into the pure air and fresh breeze blowing off the hills. With no hint of 'mare tails' over the main divide, things looked promising for another good day tomorrow.

I was after tahr.

For me this hunt was to be a standard overnight trip to shoot some meat for the freezer. Hunting in the raw, the searching out and killing of game for food — the prime stuff of being a hunter.

I really rate tahr meat. I'm not talking about some old bull tahr but, as with most game animals, I would be targeting young animals. With these being mobbed up, I was hopeful of a full pack on my walk out. So it was that I loaded up with just the bare essentials, locked the car and hid the keys under a not-so-nearby rock.

Soon enough I was over the fence and settling into a slow but steady climb up the open tussock, heading for a high terrace. I'd been into this valley before from a different route and had come out this way, realizing then how good that route would be to get me quickly back into where the game hung out.

It was typical country for South Canterbury: big expansive tussock slopes laced with matagouri and the odd gully with some sparse beech forest. At this time of day the land was cooling down and a zephyr of a breeze moved around the slopes with a tinge of coolness coming off the high ranges that still carried some patches of snow. It was late spring and I'd grabbed a quick getaway from some contract work in Christchurch to motor up here for a jaunt into the hills. It was midweek, so I was pretty hopeful that I'd be the only person in the general area. Unfortunately, I hadn't been able to get away from town until mid-afternoon, so the pressure was now on to gain some altitude and get back into the hunting ground.

The pitch of the hill had increased now but my breathing was finding some second wind, so I climbed at a good steady rate. 'Slow and steady' is my motto and before long I'd earned a breather and was able to look back and take in the reward of the views my altitude had claimed. Out to the east I could look down on the lake and way out to the Canterbury Plains, while to the west the high alps glistened with the late afternoon sun on their snow caps.

I climbed on … upwards; ever upwards. It was good to feel the system ticking over, and even though the heart muscle was working at higher revs I could feel the power in it and my legs showed no signs of weariness. Testimony, I knew, to the regular exercise I kept back home on the hills around Nelson, as well as the very light and basic kit on my back.

The broad plan was to get high and as far back into this

catchment as I could before nightfall and then be up on the ridge around dawn so that I could check catchments on both sides to locate some mobs of tahr. If you're high, you've got the drop on tahr in my opinion. Of course, at this time of year, tahr are feeding low down and I knew I could just as easily run into animals in the matagouri, so I made sure I kept scanning ahead as I angled around the slope on a course for a low point on the ridge.

The sun had left the high peaks and darkness was creeping over the upper slopes as I finally decided to bed down for the night. There is no drama for me in this regard and within a few moments I came upon a couple of metres of even ground along a contour. Soon enough the cocoon bivvy was out, the ultra-light Therm-a-Rest inside, along with the Macpac Pinnacle sleeping bag. As this bag has down only on the topside, I stripped off my one sweaty layer and got my other couple of dry layers on and climbed into the bivvy bag; which was already showing the wetness of a heavy dew settling on the alpine grasslands.

I lay in my warm little enclosure peering out the side at the stars appearing in the night sky and thinking how I'd soak up the solitude and beauty of this personal time … but I must have just dozed off! Somewhere in the night I felt quite cold and woke up so I decided to zip up the bivvy bag somewhat, but still leaving a little bit of ventilation as condensation can be a problem otherwise. I did have a bit of trouble getting back to sleep but finally must have nodded off again, for the next thing I remember was waking with that sense of a new day being already upon me.

Damn, I can't have heard the alarm on my watch. Again I regretted buying the Suunto watch, as the alarm has never been loud enough for me, even though I did value the altimeter and barometer functions. I slid out of the bag to a very wet and chilly morning — not that it was raining, but rather I was completely enshrouded in a soaking fog, with visibility down to just a few metres.

I switched back into the clammy cold of my hiking layer and quickly hauled on my rain jacket and overtrousers to cut some of the damp chill. Everything was drenched, but thankfully only a small part of the foot of my sleeping bag had gotten damp. I quickly stuffed my gear back into their bags and threw on my Macpac and set off up the hill, munching on an OSM bar for breakfast.

Direction finding was not really an issue, as I knew from the following evening that I was directly below the low point on the ridge and so I just had to climb. Within a few steps the overtrousers were sopping from pushing through the waterlogged tussock. While I was relatively dry inside, the important thing was I was protected from the fresh breeze that had developed. This breeze was quite cool, carried along in the wetness of the fog and it was some relief to reach the ridge with signs of the fog layer breaking up at this altitude.

I still had minimal visibility, so I decided to push on along the ridge to gain some more height and hopefully get above the fog. (The difference between fog and mist is the degree of visibility and this was improving now.) I felt incredible. The body was limber and idling over as I trod along the open ridgeline with swirls of mist on both sides. I was in my own world up there.

148

Climbing up through the fog on the ridge. *Emma Caigou*

The higher I went the more the mist started to dissipate and I caught glimpses of vivid blue appearing ahead of me. Yee-haa. I knew I was in for one of those great views, high above the fog-shrouded valleys.

149

Suddenly, I was out of it, stepping instantly into the cusp of a world with whiteness at my feet and a clear blue panorama above. Mountain peaks poked above the fluff and the rock ridge reached out before me like a stairway to the sky. It was pure magic.

Glorious.

I stopped and slowly rotated 360 degrees, soaking in the scene as patches of mist drifted by. I thought about grabbing my camera but then decided not to. I just lingered there instead, taking it all in and burning the image into my mind. I can see it now, as I write.

When I'd had my fill I started moving again … back to the hunt. I climbed steadily along the ridge keeping a watchful eye ahead and periodically easing off the ridge to check out the nearby country as the mist started to break up. I was peering down at one particular point, with the sun high at my back, when I noticed a bright yellow circle on some mist below. Yes, there was the shadow of a monster-man forming … the 'spectre of the Brocken'.

How good was that!

I'd had this happen to me many years previously and here, again, I was witnessing the phenomenon, where my shadow was projected below in an unusual and magnified triangular shape, with a glowing halo all around. I played with the illusion, making large arm-waving movements and bringing the 'ghost' to life. It was fun and I was like a little child discovering shadows for the first time and seeing what kind of shapes I could make. I danced left, I hopped to the right and the phantom 'mimicked' me with all sorts of trickery in its shape. I didn't want to miss any of it and so I tarried there for some time as the mist came and went below me, while the spectre dissolved and reappeared several times. Eventually, I got out my camera and attempted a photo — a poor effort at capturing a special moment in the mountains that day.

I danced and played with the phantom 'spectre of the Brocken'. *Greig Caigou*

151

With the day warming up now and the mist settled in the valley below I worked my way along the broken ridgeline. Then I caught a movement ahead, moving through the rocks at a lower level. I ducked behind a large rock, right on the main ridge. I knew I was out of sight above, so I scurried along just off the skyline to close the gap on whatever was moving my way. As I crossed the top of a steep gutter I saw them. Bulls.

The animals moved through underneath me, completely unaware of my presence in the top of the gut. They were moving along steadily and as soon as they were out of sight I hot-footed it back along in the same direction as they were headed, being careful not to dislodge any stones from on high. At the next gap I saw the tail end bull just going out of sight over into the next rock gut and so I picked up my pace to try to get a better look at their size.

Within a few minutes I was peering down into the next gully as the three bulls sidled around into full view. The lead bull looked pretty good with a bleached white mane and good rise of horn. I noted their pace had slowed somewhat and the animals started to graze on the sparse vegetation in among the rocks. They were about 50 metres below me and I put the scope on the bigger animal to check him over. At that range he looked good through six-power Leupold optics but was not the big bull that still eludes me to this day. He'd keep.

I eased back out of view and quickly rummaged for my camera in the top of the pack. Out of sight and working down through the rocks I figured I could close the gap and get a few good shots in. I checked the camera settings to make sure the shutter speed was going to be fast, with a good aperture, and

152

then I eased into view. The bigger bull was directly below me, nosing into something among the rocks. I seized the moment to grab a couple more steps to the side so as to get a better photo, when suddenly it was all over.

The bull must have sensed something or caught the movement somehow and with absolutely no warning he just took off — no standing up and checking what I was, no whistle; nothing but a hurried exit out of there!

I watched as the bulls charged down through the rocks, their manes flaring at each landing as they leapt along in full flight. Down the crags and out onto the tussock they galloped, picking up another bull along the way that had suddenly materialized out of the bottom of a creekbed. They didn't stop till they were about a kilometre away. And that was that.

Back to the business at hand: procuring some meat.

I climbed the short distance back onto the ridge and retraced my earlier steps along the ridge. I was gaining altitude towards a high point and could see no reason to have to go up and over, so started sidling around to the right. Immediately I started running into old sign. I was in the right place.

Checking my altimeter, I realized I was probably right in among the upper feed range of the animals and possibly the area they bedded down to spend the day before making their descent in the late afternoon. Quite probably, then, they were feeding up somewhere below me, so with some care I started angling down and around, keeping a good eye out on any new country. This was the right tactic and before long I caught the movement of an animal.

There they were, a whole bunch of nannies, feeding in a

sunny hollow in among some rocks. Again I had the drop on the animals, so I eased back and took off my pack to get the camera out. This time I checked all the camera settings as well as putting a round up the spout of the .270. It was time for some action.

Nanny tahr — meat on the hoof. *Michael McClunie*

I crouched and shuffled forward to a large rock to check on the animals and, yes, they were still nose down in the low tussock. I figured the next large rock ahead would offer a good spot for a picture and a rest for the rifle and so eased across some open ground to that, keeping my eye out for any animals that might raise the alarm. When I checked out from this next rock I saw I was in a good position at around 30 metres from the mob. There was plenty of light to allow good aperture and shutter speed and the mist still in the valley below would be an excellent backdrop. With only a 70 mm lens I reckoned to close the gap even more and get some really good photos.

That was my undoing — again.

When I shuffled out from the other side of the rock to make for a closer vantage point I was immediately spotted by an unseen nanny coming over a small rise, not 20 metres away. It bolted straight away and I knew the game was up.

Forget the photo.

The camera was promptly laid aside and I rocketed forward to a handy vantage point and slammed myself down prone over the top of it while trying to follow the closest animal as the mob charged off down the guts below. There were maybe 20 or so animals dashing everywhere, but I wasn't counting; I was totally focused on looking for a beast that was still working its way towards an escape route.

I hurriedly found one and planted the scope on him, closing the bolt and settling in solidly behind the butt. I traced along with the animal and imagined its route as the scope's field of view sent back clues of what lay ahead. And yes, here it was, coming up to a pause — that fatal pause to suss out the next place to run into, a pause that was enough for the trigger to release and the shot to be away.

The tahr collapsed instantly, cartwheeling over the side of the little rock it was on and into the steep gutter.

I worked the bolt and scanned around for another, but the shot had given impetus to their mad dash and any further long-range shots seemed pointless.

I sure gave them the hurry up, but it had turned out a bit of a debacle really.

I slammed myself for not being satisfied with my first position when in close to that mob. Just a tad cocky, I thought. Oh well, tahr number one was on the ground at least and I reckoned I'd pulled off a good quick shot of around 150 metres when under pressure. The meat had to be got, so I rounded up my camera and pack and left them in a prominent spot before clambering down to the tahr. The animal turned out to be a yearling male and would make excellent eating.

Back up on the ridge again I settled down on a prominent rock and munched on another OSM while enjoying the ocean of white fluff below me.

Soon enough I continued on my way, sticking at that altitude. The amount of sign about indicated that I was traversing at the right level and I still had time to intercept animals before they bedded down for the day.

About an hour later I again managed to catch a movement on a rocky spine, some way ahead, so I hunkered down against a rock to glass the area. Sure enough, I had picked up a small group of nannies settling into their midday lair, high on a rock ledge.

This time I wasn't going to get too concerned about a photograph and so began a stalk to take me towards a good shooting platform from which I could cover the expanse of the rock garden. I worked my way down and into a gut before scrambling up the other side lower down and within range of the four nannies. At about 200 metres I settled on a flattish section of the spur and got my pack off to use as a support for the stock. The animals were bedded down below me, totally unaware of the hunter focusing in on them from above.

I took my time, letting my breathing slow right down to a steady rise and fall in the sight picture. When all was ready I took my finger off the trigger guard and eased it into the comfort spot on the trigger. All was set: good and deadly.

When my breathing paused the 130 grain was away and the mountains boomed with the blast from the .270. The tahr slumped over and the response was immediate from the other animals as they bounded forward onto the rocky rib where I'd first caught their movement. Working the bolt as quickly as all this occurred, the crosshairs settled on a second animal and the shot banged out immediately. I saw the tahr leap forward, dead on his feet and plummeting headlong over into a gully. I lifted my head looking for another animal and followed it as it scrambled around, not sure where to run. The crosshairs found their mark in the middle of the chest — but I didn't fire. That was enough for today.

I gathered up my shells, checked the magazine and closed the bolt on an empty chamber. I was done, happy with good, clean kills. Happy to have been firing some shots again.

I cut down to the animals and set about my butchering. The load was getting heavy now and with my bivvy bag on the outside, along with my parka, I had managed to get all the meat inside the pack. Though there was some weight to it, I resolved to clamber back up to the ridge and continue on a bit further, so that I could connect with an easier looking slope for a descent. At the same time this would allow me a chance to look over into an adjacent basin for future reference.

And so it was that at around two o'clock I paused my travelling, nestling into a small sheltered hollow up under the main ridge and drifted off into the snooze of a fully satisfied hunter.

Take time to enjoy the local flora. *Greig Caigou*

When I awoke it was so quiet and still way up there. I was out of the light breeze and only if I listened really hard could I hear any distant sounds of the mountains, perhaps the creek way down below or the breeze caressing the tussock slopes.

I eased my body back to life and lazily unfurled before having a good long stretch, like some yoga master tweaking each joint along the spinal column. Climbing into my harness, I gathered up my rifle and ever so slowly set off on the short pitch to the ridge. Gradually, the tempo lifted and before long I was moving along at a good clip, making for a bend in the ridge that I surmised would provide a good vantage point to check over the head basin of the adjacent watershed.

Having settled into a comfy spot I got busy with the binoculars and it wasn't long before I picked up animals. There was a bull way out under a solitary outcrop of rock, right in the middle of the head basin, about a kilometre away. There appeared to be a small group of nannies a little further around, but it was hard to know how many were there, as I think some were still bedded down. It was close to the magic hour late in the afternoon, so I assumed more animals would materialize as I continued my searching.

Sure enough, as I scanned around to the face straight opposite me I picked up movement and focused in on that. On the other side of the valley, at the head of an expansive tussock slope, some animals were descending out of the rock spines that ran up to the ridge. At first I picked up half a dozen but as I watched, more and more animals converged into the same general area and before long I counted 37 tahr in the group.

It was wonderful to watch as they fed around while making their descent. Some would have a little chase of each other and others ambled along, not much interested in the food as yet. There were a few bulls present in the mob and I guessed they were younger animals, but the herd was largely made up of nannies and their young, as a nursery group. I kept my eye on their progress while checking over some other likely spots in the headwaters, but nothing else was seen. These animals would keep for another day of meat shooting (perhaps). Choppers or no choppers, I was exercising my own personal code of taking only what I needed.

If we hunters could be left alone to handle game manage-ment, especially on this easily accessed front country, three or four hunters taking half a dozen animals a year could maintain a sustainable supply of wild meat in this small area. This could be the case in every other catchment, too, where tahr numbers build up. Of course, more hunters will have to value game meat and make the effort to harvest and use wild food, rather than just rolling it down the hill or only targeting mature males.

Just some of the mighty fine tahr salami. *Greig Caigou*

Time to go. I'd had my fill of animals in the wild and I'd got what I had come for, so I turned to make tracks for home.

Back over the ridge and straight down the tussock slope that I had eyed up earlier. This was easy going and before long I was at the creek and taking my fill of the effervescent and sharply cold water. Onwards I trudged, enjoying just being out there.

And then it occurred to me.

I don't really have to be out tonight! My next job is a full day away. What's the rush to get out and back to Christchurch? Why not stop and camp here? What's stopping me sleeping under the stars, with the sound of a babbling creek beside me and all those other favourite things?

Ahh … those favourite things.

I tarried there. My solo camping arrangement. *Greig Caigou*

The work and feeling the body ticking over. Some hardship of the cold night under the heavy dew. Magic moments earned atop the ridge as nature turned on the scenery. Some play with the phantom 'spectre'. The wide, open spaces and getting in close to wild animals. The thrill of shooting and the thump of solid kills ... meat on the hoof. Camping out. Solitary — in the mountains.

The day had it all for me.

So I camped right there; soaking it all in and grabbing as much of it as I could — while I could!

Chapter 7

Jansen Travis — hunt hard

'So what's a stand-out, classic hunting memory for you, Jansen?'

There was absolutely no hesitation to his reply. 'Shooting my first bull tahr, on a hunt with Dad.'

Jansen takes up the story:

I was 14 at the time and we'd headed off from Loburn, in North Canterbury, for the Queen's Birthday weekend. The plan was to hunt up on Godley Peaks Station and get as far up the valley as possible on the Friday night, so we would be in a good spot for hunting on the first day. There was Dad as well as Johnny and his father John. Johnny was a rugby mate and I've done most of my hunting with him ever since, as he shares my hunting values and loves a good hard day on the hill.

It was really cold riding up the valley on the quad bike. We boys rode in the trailer with the gear and I remember hunkering down around the gear to get out of the chill — but it was still freezing. I was sure glad to get to Ribbonwood Hut, especially as it was snowing heavily by that stage. It was so cold, that even after lighting the fire in the small hut, it didn't seem to be much warmer and the temperature plummeted outside. When we turned off the gas lantern that night it cooled so quickly that the glass shattered!

It was a pretty long night for me sleep-wise, as I was kept awake with the cold and I was still pretty excited about going on my first tahr hunt as well. By this stage I'd shot several deer and plenty of small game, as well as going out heaps with Dad on pig hunting trips, but I'd not been back into the alps to shoot tahr or chamois. I could hardly wait.

Next day we were up before dawn and off for the day, climbing high up the spur on the true right of Ribbonwood Stream, with Johnny and his dad heading up the true left opposite us. I followed Dad's footsteps up the hill and as it got lighter it dawned reasonably clear but was still overcast and really chilly, with a cool wind coming straight off the snow. I could barely wait for the sun to come up, because even with the work of climbing I was still quite cold.

Eventually, though, we got up high enough. I was just so blown away with all the scenery. It was great to be up there, up high, with mountains all around. I think that helped spark my love for the more alpine high country.

We did a lot of looking through the binos once we got up to that height, but we didn't see anything. We started to sidle along the hillside in the soft snow, heading towards the head of the gully where Dad thought the tahr might be hanging out. Tahr love rock and the steep stuff, but I've never been scared following Dad into these areas.

We didn't come onto any tahr and so we just kept sidling along the face, keeping our eyes open as we came into each new gut. We'd check up the face and down each spur and progressed along like this all day. I don't even remember stopping for lunch; we just kept moving and that's pretty much the style of hunting I'd gotten used to with my father. To this day he still hunts this way and I struggle to keep up with him. *[Darrell is 53 years young.]*

Darrell is a keen hunter. Jansen's dad with a hefty load on. *Jansen Travis*

My dad loves the challenge of hunting and I know I picked that up from him. Success was about how much work you put in. So it's physical — and its always a hard day when I hunt with Dad. Sometimes, when most others are ready to turn for home, he'll start off in some other direction and all I can think is: 'Oh no, shit, what's he up to now?' He'll be off to check just one more spot. That really puts the edge on his success rate; he'll do a different thing: go earlier, go longer and when after these alpine animals he'll always go higher, as tahr never seem to look up!

Really late in the day, about an hour before dark, Dad said, 'We'll do one more gully.'

I was poked, but off he went, with me plugging along behind him. In my earlier years I'd had real trouble with these longer trips on the hill and was suffering heaps, but once it got figured out that I had asthma, I was away. I'd been feeling a bit low, though, on this day because we'd ploughed through that snow for hours and each new gully had failed to deliver on any promise of seeing tahr. However, the thought of only one more gully was a bit of a lift because then we could head on back to the hut and have a decent feed.

As the snow was getting hard on top by now, we carefully sidled around into a big shingle chute with vertical bluffs above it. There was a sheer drop on our side as well and I said to Dad, 'You wouldn't see tahr here, would you?'

Dad replied, 'You'd be surprised.'

I looked further over the edge and straight away I saw a big black animal just above the slip on the vertical face. It was the first tahr I had ever seen. It just stood out so easily and straight away we knew we were looking at a big bull. What a sight!

This was always going to be my first shot, so Dad helped me get into position. We were straight across from the bull at about 150 yards, so it was fairly easy to set up a nice rest, laying the rifle across a clump of snowgrass. When I lined up the bull in the scope he just looked awesome and my heart was really thumping by then. Dad kept telling me to take my time and was talking me through the shot. He told me to line up on the middle of the chest. I was using an old Swedish Mauser action 6.5 x 55 that had a double trigger pressure, so I had to squeeze in on the trigger till it came back, taking up the first pressure.

'Now hold it there, watch your breathing, get real steady ... take your time.'

My heart was pounding but I kept hearing Dad in my ear.

'Take your time.'

And then the shot punched out, noise exploding all around — and straight away, as the scope shocked back into position, I could see the tahr do a big leap and crash down off the rocks into the gut.

I got him!

Suddenly, there were tahr everywhere. They just burst from the face — I couldn't get over that. Where did they all come from? We counted 18 as they scrambled out of there and down the hill. Dad didn't even raise his firearm at any. We'd got what we were after; I'd got my bull and that was it.

(I still admire that about Dad. I think he developed his ethics by hunting through the tough times when few animals were about and having plenty of success over the years. He never shot anything unless there was a reason, just like he'd never let me shoot hinds, as they were deemed to be breeding stock. I can remember during a roar hunt we saw a good chamois buck and I was eager to shoot it, but he'd turned to me and said, 'We are here for a stag, aren't we?' That's all that was said.)

When we got over to the bull tahr it was just such a fantastic feeling to have shot one. Dad was as ecstatic as I was, maybe even more so. It was big and pretty heavy and we heaved it around into position for a photo. (We later measured the head at 12½ inches.)

By the time we did the business cutting off the head and grabbing the skin it was getting late, so we set off straight down the shingle gut on a fast descent to the matagouri and then pushed through that out onto the valley floor. I was real hungry by that time, but we still had probably a full hour of trudging down the flats in the dark to the hut. As was usual, we'd had another long day, setting off maybe an hour before dark that morning and getting in after dark. Mum's bacon and egg pie was looking pretty fine for tea that night!

Johnny and his dad had shot some nannies and we all sat around, eating plenty and yarning for ages and to top it off the hut had even managed to heat up!

On our way out from that trip I remember Mrs Scott, the landowner's wife, blowing Dad up a bit for what we'd been wearing. She especially didn't think Dad's jeans or my track pants were proper hunting gear for in the mountains and probably not the rubber Ashley boots we were wearing either! But this is what Dad, his mates and I used all the time when hunting pigs and we'd gotten pretty used to handling any terrain in those things. And, besides, now I could claim my first bull tahr, shot in the snow in the Southern Alps — while wearing track pants and rubber boots!

I first met Jansen via the online forum of the social networking site at fishnhunt (www.fishnhunt.co.nz).

This is a great place to connect with other active hunters. If you search back through the thousands of threads you can get all manner of advice and tips about hunting, gear, terrain and the like, as well as all sorts of opinionated commentary on issues that affect our outdoor life — among other things!

As a forum 'senior', Jansen (avatar 'Stag') had organized a hunt for forum members into South Westland and had spent considerable time sorting logistics in order to provide a relatively cheap airlift into the country around the Whataroa catchment. We'd all met online but it was somewhat nerve-racking to finally connect with everyone at the Whataroa Pub and put faces to names and measure each other up — over a beer. Of course, everyone turned out to be real friendly and among the hard cases and experienced hunters were others, looking for their first big adventure into these alps. Jansen had organized teams so that some of these new chums could link up with hunters who could pass on experience and some know-how. It was great to see the sort of camaraderie develop among people who were prepared to assist others in this regard.

We had atrocious weather on that trip and most parties were tent or hut-bound for much of the planned five days. In fact most parties, including the group I was in, flew out earlier than planned; before the next wave of incoming fronts held us in there longer than our leave from work permitted.

Even from that first encounter, I'd have to describe Jansen as generous! He has been immeasurably helpful to those who have asked him for all sorts of information, especially to newer chums starting out and wanting to shoot their first tahr or chamois. He's taken out some of these newcomers and got them their first animals, too. Hunting is somewhat evolving for Jansen at the moment; in the early days it was all about having a shoot-up, whereas now he really enjoys watching others score.

I asked Jansen what he likes in his own hunting now.

'Getting out there, I guess; the camaraderie. I'm also quite competitive, though, competing against the animals and getting in on them. That doesn't mean I have to put a bullet in them; I just like to know I've gotten the drop on them. I'm still after the big red stag, though ... the dream head, that super big one that's got no farming influence in them! I wouldn't be satisfied with shooting a stag that just came from an area known to produce scrappy heads and yet all of a sudden some great big trophy head appears there. I'd want a bona fide animal that hasn't had any outside influence in it, and it would have to come off public land.'

Jansen is a networker, too, and seems to know so many different people, especially back-country farm owners (which in part has come about through his job with Beef and Lamb New Zealand). Jansen also has that most useful of skills in being able to get to the centre of an issue quickly, cutting through all the ramblings or less important dross to nail down the real issues or sticking points of a discussion. And then, he's not afraid to speak his mind. On the other hand, he doesn't like a lot of the stuff around the politics of the sport, as it just takes the edge off hunting. Ask him about an issue such as heli-hunting and he recoils with: 'Guided heli-hunting on public lands is just plain offensive — they've got safari parks for that kind of nonsense!'

Jansen reckons his dad tried to get him out hunting as soon as possible. *Jansen Travis*

Jansen grew up in Loburn and went to Rangiora High School. By that stage he'd shot his first deer and pigs with his father's old .270. He had also stuck plenty of pigs (sticking his first pig when around six years old). He had done a heap of hunting with his dad and was getting pretty good on the end of a firearm as well.

Jansen and Johnny carry out their first deer — at age 13. *Jansen Travis*

In those years at high school he was starting to earn good pocket money shooting hares and rabbits at night. These were worth $1.60 a kilogram and he'd be shooting 15 or 20 a night. He continued shooting rabbits with his mate Johnny during summer breaks and regularly shot and skinned over 380 a night. He took a year off after his first year at university and as a 19 year old worked full-time shooting hares and rabbits, making between $250 and $500 a night (which was good money in those days). He loved the high country and working in that environment.

Shooting hares for pocket money. *Jansen Travis*

Jansen fits well with the generational theme of this book because he's just come up 30 years old and so slots into that 'Gen X' period between my Baby Boomer age group and the younger Gen Y'ers. His generation tends to be independent, resourceful, self-sufficient and values freedom and flexibility, where they can work hard and then go play hard. Certainly, Jansen works hard, both at his job and at his hunting.

Interestingly, though, while Jansen works hard when hunting, he would not describe himself as a lean, mean 'athletic-machine'; however, he does possess that enduring ability to just keep going! Fitness, in my humble opinion, is as much about mental toughness and resolve as it is about resting heart rates, cardiovascular capacity, speed and strength, for example. Stamina on the hills is that ability to be still going at the end of the day — and then some! We hunters can often still be at it well after other outdoors folk might be tucked up in their sleeping bags or playing cards in the hut. Also our packs are often heavier on the way out from a trip than when hiking in!

This kind of endurance only comes from time on the hills, building an inner capacity that just gets on with it and knowingly accepts that long days on the legs, in thick scrub and tricky terrain with big loads, is all part of the game anyway. Consistently plodding along gets the job done in good time and is the kind of hunter-fitness we should aim for, in my opinion.

Jansen has played grade and representative rugby as a No. 7 openside flanker for many years, but it was the foundational grounding of long days out with his dad that has forged the level of toughness that has helped him in his sport as well as in his hunting nowadays.

'You have to push yourself and use your binos heaps, but when it comes down to it you've got to put in the yards,' he says.

174

Jansen is there, too, on the job at the end of the day, when others might be too tired. Long days hunting, camp life and self-reliance have a way of dictating that the shelter will not put itself up nor will the hunger satisfy itself. The work still has to be done in that respect, despite how you feel.

He hunts with a variety of weapons and has been known to lug around a big bang-stick of 14.2 pounds (that's 6.4 kg). The calibre is 6.5-284 and he pushes 140-grain A-Max projectiles along at over 3000 fps. Jansen is currently having a lighter version of this rifle built, for quite a few dollars!

His favourite weapon, however, is still his trusty Browning A-Bolt in .270 calibre and he's pretty much shot everything he's got with that rifle.

Some other interesting features about Jansen's set-up for hunting, at this stage in his life, would be his use of an Aarn pack when on the hills. While a bit unusual to get into, these packs rely on having some of the weight of your gear loaded on the front shoulder straps in order to counter-balance the weight on your back and assist the wearer to a more natural walking position. These packs are not that well set up for humping out big weights of meat, but they are of a capacity that many more hunters should aspire to in the sense of some better rationalization of the excess gear they lug around in the hills. Personally, I prefer a single-compartment, lighter-weight canvas pack with no-nonsense features; Macpac's Ravine pack fits the bill especially well for me. (You can check out the Cactus packs too and for a good price the guys at Twin Needle in Christchurch put together a customizable variation of these other canvas packs.)

In my first book I had something to say about more ultra-light habits as far as gear and the techno-stuff we hunters carry. Increasingly, this is an area where outdoors people are assailed with pressure to add ever more sophisticated stuff to their basic kit. The more often I do without something in the hills the more often I surprise myself with how I don't miss that item and get by perfectly well without it … thank you very much!

Some of the best hunters I've seen in action have very little in the way of sophisticated gear, carry minimal other stuff and yet are extremely efficient in bagging game. There's always going to be more and better gear to add to our kits. We just have to be careful that we take advantage of new or lightweight advances in clothing systems, for example, without taking more and more trinkets that offset any gains made in terms of lightness or highly portable gear.

Find out what you absolutely must have in the outdoors and then learn to work well with that.

There are also little features that hunters develop for themselves to help their efficiency. I liked the innovation that Jansen has of a dog clip on a short length of webbing from the base of his pack. He can then hang his weapon over his neck and shoulder and tuck the rifle stock in close to his side. This allows him to freely truck along at a good steady pace with the weight of his rife snugly contained. In many instances you are just portaging the weapon and once in a stalking position, the rifle can be unclipped and carried in a state of readiness. This is especially true for alpine hunters.

For me, I like to carry my weapon in my hand, but for those longer periods of just getting somewhere, the arrangement used by Jansen is useful. I also find my rifle real handy as an extra support when hill climbing and it is often deployed to assist on the steep stuff, or as I start to get wearier!

Jansen and 'Mr Stick' — happy in the back-country. *Jansen Travis*

In this regard Jansen was the first person I had hunted with who used a walking pole or stick. So while his musket was clipped alongside, Jansen would move along with 'Mr Stick' as a third leg. It did impress me that this set-up meant that in combination with his Aarn pack, he was able to walk in an upright walking position that was well balanced, even when carrying a good load. The stick came in handy for a sturdy prop on water crossings, downhill on variable terrain and also as a stake which you plant firmly and hoist up on while climbing in search of game. Of course, musterers and high country folk have used a sturdy pole for years in the back-country, and modern-day trampers, walkers and alpinists use two lightweight poles for more Nordic style, cross-country backpacking. The theory is that there is less impact on the knees and better all-round support with the extra 'leg' provided. Poles are also supposed to help you keep more upright in your stance. I saw the theory in practice with this hunter and was impressed.

Jansen uses a small, lighter manuka pole than the thick ones used by musterers and at times, if the stick was in the way, it was easy to toss it down a small drop-off or poke through the scrub. I guessed, too, that 'Mr Stick' had been with Jansen often enough as it had become an extension of himself. (I suspect that I'd forget to pick mine up again after a rest stop and leave the pole behind!)

Some other gear refinements are worth picking up on while on this topic.

Jansen has spent some time on the fishnhunt forum gathering intel from other hunters on items as broad-ranging as bivvy tentage to outer shell clothing. (It was good to see some of my recommendations being taken up also and Jansen now uses more alpine-style rainwear versus the heavier soft shell jackets popular with the hunting retailers.) Jansen has picked the eyes out of the advice on the forum when it comes to his other gear as well and trialled the super lightweight Siltarps before he settled on a lightweight one-person tent.

For me, one of the disadvantages of the cocoon arrangement I mentioned in my first book is that cooking or changing clothes is awkward in poor weather when just relying on a one-person bivvy bag. It's not always easy or possible to find a spot under a rock to camp, and a fly gives that extra dry space in such conditions. If you're hunting solo and using a one-person bivvy bag, you don't then want to add a standard-weight fly as well. The combined weight might be more than just taking a tent or at least a tent fly! For this reason something like the 200-gram Siltarp provides a good degree of extra protection and is made of tough parachute-style nylon.

We hunters are constantly reviewing our gear and this is increasingly so as technology moves forward with improvements coming available every year. It's important for hunters to constantly check what others are using; the networking sites for hunters, trampers and mountaineers make for very useful reading. This is especially so for newer hunters. It's also invaluable when you can get alongside other hunters out in the field and see different ways of working, and for this reason I've found it really useful to sometimes leave my solo hunting ways and get out on the hills with someone else. The challenge is to not get caught up in buying more and more gear and believing that will supplant good old-fashioned skill learnt in the field.

When hunting with Jansen I came to appreciate the skills he had built up behind his binoculars as well. Some people, like my fishing friend Grant, are just naturals at spotting game. While time out on the hills spent looking is beneficial and while good optics help (Jansen uses Swarovski binos), there are just some people who spot game easily. Jansen is one of them, and I found him exceptionally quick at being able to locate game. Looking in the right places helps, knowing the colours to look for helps, too, but at the end of the day some people just don't see half the game that is on the hill and this is a skill to be admired.

Jansen honed these skills from an early age and much credit should be given to his dad, Darrell, for getting out with his boy on adventures. (His first forays out hunting with his father started from age three, while propped up in a pack on Darrell's back!) While this memorable hunt for the bull tahr was special for the kill of his first big alpine animal, Jansen feels the classic aspect of this New Zealand hunting adventure was that his dad was there with him. It was his father who had introduced him to hunting and had encouraged him by taking him along on pig hunts and later when he let Jansen loose to go shoot hares.

Jansen recalls one special heart-pounding hunt with his father, out after roaring stags in the Puketeraki Range of North Canterbury. They were in the bush and his dad was roaring up a stag. Darrell was doing such a good job of mimicking a randy stag that he roared the thing in from two kilometres away. It just kept coming. Jansen could see the antlers moving up through the bush, and as the stag poked its head around the side of a tree, Jansen was able to shoot it from close range, right between the eyes!

He has had many other such memorable moments out hunting since that special trip where he shot the bull tahr with his dad alongside him. Jansen still considers Darrell his best mate for spending time with in the hills.

Good on ya — both!

Chapter 8

Alpine days close to home

It was just another one of those glorious days high on the main ridge and that favourite moment for me of cresting the rise and shuffling a few metres off the skyline to huddle into a spotting position. My eyes scanned near and far checking for any obvious animals before I wriggled myself into a more solid arrangement and pulled out the binoculars that hung down inside my lightweight jacket.

The small hollows of the likely looking country were studied through the binos for some time and periodically I swung the glasses over the more expansive country, just in case an animal was way out in the open. I recalled this had been the case the last time I was in this basin. While examining all the likely spots, a chamois had suddenly appeared right out in the middle of a shingle scree, as bold as could be. But there was nothing that leapt into view today, so I shuffled somewhat and started again to peer into some creek heads that were a way down below to my left.

And then, there they were. Chamois.

I found the chamois feeding on the edge of a little gut just below where the upper slopes of the basin spilled down through some steep gutters. I love this moment of finding game after all the hard work of getting into the alpine meadows and then watching them go about their life, oblivious to the hunter's gaze high above.

This classic day had begun at 3 a.m. as I eased out of bed and slipped quietly down the hall to the kitchen, where I'd dumped my hunting clothes the night before. While the jug boiled I quickly dressed and scoffed down some Hubbard's muesli and yoghurt at the same time. I thought it wise to fuel up some more so a piece of bread went in the toaster while this was all happening. Before long a lavish layer of peanut butter and honey was being force fed between sips of hot tea. In what were really only a few minutes I was sneaking back down the hall and out the front door to the car. (I'd left this out of the garage so as not to disturb my wife too much in the early hours with the door opening.)

The night sky was the first thing I checked and the sparkling stars confirmed the forecast I'd checked on MetVUW the night before. Clear skies — the promise of another beaut Nelson day.

The drive up towards Nelson Lakes is just right for a day's hunt out of Nelson. You gradually leave the little hamlets of civilization, such as Brightwater and Wakefield, and gain speed up through the pine forests before cresting Reay Saddle. Immediately, your eyes can pick up the outlines of high mountains away to the south and the excitement starts to build. By then the car is good and warm and the growing sense of solitude is kicking back in.

In a little over an hour I had turned off up a side road and parked up, with the warmth of the car enticing me to linger there, especially given the sharp coolness of the morning outside. I was there to hunt, but it sometimes takes a while to adjust to the contrasting mode of crisp air and the work required to gain the high tops.

With an abrupt awakening from my comfort zone I opened the door and made ready for the work ahead.

The climb up onto the tops was surprisingly easy and I kept a consistent pace up the valley in the darkness, with just the headlamp to light my way. Fitness is such a key to enjoying these days on the hills and I was glad for those two or three times a week I kept my base fitness up with runs or hill climbs up behind Richmond. (I was always leaner and fitter in these summer and autumn months anyway because I was just that much more active over the long days.) Soon I took to the steeper pitch up to the bushline and again I worked away at a slow but consistent climb. I've found this works best for me — drop the body into crawler gear but just keep at it. With few rest stops I made good time gaining altitude towards the tussock.

Dawn was upon the tops and after just over an hour I was at the bush edge and quietly sneaking around to get a variety of views out onto the close grasslands, just in case a deer might be caught out feeding. With nothing spotted I moved out into the open and worked my way up a depression to a small knob where I knew there was a good view over the adjacent basin where I'd hunted once before.

I spent time glassing there before moving on diagonally around the slope and up towards some nasty guts that slashed down off the main ridge. I'd not been in this part of the valley before and about this time some fog rolled in and I was completely enfolded with whiteness. It was quite disorientating as I climbed through this unfamiliar terrain, but I could manage around 50 metres of visibility and thought it quite possible that I might come upon some chamois as I sidled through the tops of these guts.

Tops hunter. The author waiting for a clearance. *Greig Caigou*

The fog was quite wetting, so I'd donned my lightweight Macpac jacket and pushed on towards the main ridge where I arrived in virtually zero visibility. This was not working out and I had to get around to more familiar country and some breeze to hopefully break up the fog.

After some sidling I dropped over the side into another basin. With encouraging signs of the fog breaking up in this part of the tops I was soon heading for the edge of a prominent spur that would give me a good view into the next basin. I had arrived at high altitude under cover of the fog and would have the drop on any animals down below. The day was starting to shape up to be a good one.

The six chamois below me appeared to be holding in the one feeding area so I figured they would spend most of the day there, resting up. It was a perfect position, hidden from any approach directly above and with full view of all the valley and basin below. More importantly, this position allowed the chamois to catch any scent carried up the valley on the daytime thermals. But from my location I had these light breezes in my face and I was still able to look down to their position.

Now to planning the stalk.

The two best options were to cut around from my height to directly above the animals and then just drop straight down above them or to cut down through a bluff system below me and come around close under this, at the same level as the chamois. Both plans were good and I've always tended to opt for coming directly down on the animals. However, I liked the second option in this case because I figured I could come around having all animals in view and better choose which animal to shoot. Sometimes in steep guts the problem with coming down from above is that the animals are not visible until you're directly upon them, and if they're spread out you don't always have the luxury of choice before the game is up.

So with my mind tentatively made up I got myself sorted, taking off my shell jacket now that the day was fine. I also put on my camo hat to shield the shock of silver-grey hair that lights up like a beacon in the outdoors. Down through the bluffs I went at a good clip, loving the little challenges of sorting the best route through the steeper sections. Once out under the bluff system I hugged the shadow right in against the rock wall and before long came into view of the animals at around 400 metres. With a check through the binoculars I was able to identify all six chamois and I double-checked above the group in case there was some sentinel on watch for approaching danger.

Sure enough, there she was!

I'd not spotted this animal before as she must have been out of sight at the time, but now the game was up. I'd incorrectly assumed a group of three nannies each with last season's young; so six animals fitted that account. This sentinel must be an older nanny, perhaps with no offspring. I spent some time watching and checking everywhere in case there was an extra young chamois I'd missed. Eventually, I settled on the matriarch being without young and definitely the lookout for this little mob.

Holding to my course, I crawled forward, keeping a watchful eye on the sentry and only moving when she looked the other way or put her head down to rest. With this strategy I managed to close the distance to around 300 metres. The group of animals kept feeding and I watched for some time, just enjoying being with these wild creatures in their habitat.

Now I can shoot chamois at 300 metres, but I love getting

in close. I had plenty of day left and was up here for the joy of being on the tops and being with animals. There was no need to charge around looking over new country, there was no 'driven' rush to my life up here. So I just watched through the binoculars.

Chamois are a lovely animal. Sleek and graceful. Alert. Ever alert. They feed along but keep looking up, scanning around below them and when satisfied that all is safe they tuck in again on some plant. I think they are the premium game animal in New Zealand. I find tahr to have this 'attitude' about them that if they are on a bluff system then they pooh-pooh any approaching danger because they figure you can't come up to them. This is why they are so susceptible to modern long-range rifle power. A skilled marksman who knows their ballistics well can set up a good rest at a distance and knock them off their perch right out of the bluffs.

Chamois are smart and have fantastic eyesight — as well as that sixth sense that something is not quite right. Zeff Veronese reckons they're 'telepathic' and that's why you shouldn't look at them when you're stalking in close, because they can 'feel' you there! (He may be right, for hunters will know all too well that when sneaking up on a chamois under cover and peering out from behind a rock or shrub, they always seem to be looking straight at you. How do they know?)

I also love this type of chamois country, more so than places in Westland where the animals spend some time in the bush. Chamois are an alpine animal and I just love seeing them out in the kind of terrain in which I was watching this little group.

The sentinel nanny began to catch more of my interest. She

was obviously the older animal and through the binos appeared to have high horns. To take an old nanny is a real challenge, sometimes more of a challenge than an older buck. Bucks will still lose their caution during the rut; not so a nanny.

A very good set of horns taken on an earlier trip. *Greig Caigou*

With my mind made up now I started to rethink my plan so that I could target the nanny. Where she was lying down did not present a good target from my position and it was now largely open ground over to the animals. I still wanted to get in close and as the challenge of stalking this nanny had now become my goal it was back to my other option.

It seemed best to retrace my steps, climb back up through the bluffs and sidle around to come down directly above her. With a last check on the herd I turned and snuck back through the snowgrass and up into the shadow against the rock wall before taking another check on the animals. No change, so off I went along the bluff wall and into the steep slice I'd come down earlier. The heart rate climbed as I ascended through the bluffs and before long I was moving quickly across the upper slopes well above the chamois. It was important to get this part of the stalk done quickly in case the nanny made a change to her position.

I'd lined up a couple of features so that I could identify the correct spur the nanny was on and once I'd confirmed these in my mind I began to drop down. As I closed the distance and the spur dropped away below me, I began to get into stealth mode, checking and rechecking through the binos that the animal hadn't gotten up and moved position where I would be caught on the hop. Closer and closer I descended the spur. I could see a knob below me that I realized was probably where the spur dropped off more steeply; down to the place where the nanny was on watch above her herd. With my focus on making that knob I had one final check around and then shuffled down onto the point.

Sure enough, it was as I suspected and I found myself peering over the lip at the nanny bedded down some 50 metres below. But I'd looked! She lifted her head to look up the hill and I promptly averted my gaze and slid back out of sight. Maybe there is something to that telepathic sixth sense … instinct that danger is nearby?

I got my daypack off and laid it onto the knob out of view and then fed a round into the .270 and put the bolt into half-cock. I lay across the pack and took a few deep breaths to calm myself, before easing forward and tipping the barrel over the lip, angling steeply down the slope. Perhaps I'd willed my thoughts away from the animal because now she was back to looking over the feeding herd that I could see scattered among the snowgrass below.

I placed the crosshairs on the centreline of her back and then waited. All was settled. The rifle was snug and secure. My breathing calm. The animal at rest. Plenty of time.

I could have taken some photos of the animal as it lay there on its perch. I thought about it; they would have made wonderful photos, but to this day I can see every detail of that chamois in my mind's eye and sometimes that kind of memory is all you need.

For the longest time I just watched that nanny through the scope. Every detail on her well-conditioned body. I zoned in on the horns and confirmed again their length — good height above the ears and good bases for a nanny, too. I settled the crosshairs back on the darker line of her spine and watched some more. And then I fired.

Plain and simple — calculated — and without moving the animal died where she lay.

There's a certain beauty in a good shot.

The other chamois bounded around the slope a few metres

before stopping, not knowing where the danger had come from. Heads turned this way and that and I watched with amusement as at first they decided to run a few metres one way and then, changing their mind, ran back again, looking all around with a tense sense of alarm. Seldom did they look up, but when I eventually stood up I was spotted almost immediately and then they were off, making a fast getaway straight down the slopes and out into the basin at full gallop. It's still amazing watching how much distance these animals can put between themselves and danger in just a few moments.

Then the mountains were still again.

I gathered up my things and climbed down to the lifeless nanny. She lay exactly where she had been on the job as sentry — a beautiful animal — and I stood beside her gazing over her form. If I had known then of the Austrian custom of placing a last morsel in her mouth as a mark of respect, I would have done it. The horns were special and went out over nine inches with fairly good hooks and strong bases for a nanny, but more significant was the fact that she was an older animal and by my reckoning perhaps 11 years old. She had roamed these alpine meadows for a good lifetime and had no doubt reared young that were still among the chamois that lived in these ranges; and perhaps among those she watched over that day.

I was feeling it was a fitting place for the old matriarch to end her days, nestled in high under the rock outcrops of the head basin and overlooking the expansive alpine valley below; it was a spot, too, that I could visit when on another alpine jaunt.

I cut up the chamois and boned out the meat, which would certainly go well enough in the very good salami that the butcher back in Wakefield had been doing lately. It was time to turn for home and with a solid weight in my Pursuit pack I turned for the pinch up the hill to the main ridge.

The old sentinel nanny where she died. *Greig Caigou*

It was great to hear my heart beating strongly as I climbed, setting my eye on a narrow slot on the ridgeline at the head of an old rockslide. I'd fixed that as the challenge and aimed to get up there without stopping for a breather. The higher I made it the more determined I became to make the goal. I'd been keeping in pretty good shape over the last few years and I was pretty stoked at my solid climb. With a final heaving effort I stepped strongly up onto the main ridge and sucked in the clear air and the mountain views that stretched out far beyond that slot.

Time to linger. *Simon Buschl*

It was great to be up there: solid effort and good skills, a full pack of meat, body ticking over as it should be, mountain vistas ... the life of a hunter.

I headed on down the rather steep confines of the slot and out the bottom into some sweeping grass slopes, eyeing up on some small tarns over in the lip of the basin. From a distance the spot looked picnic perfect. Soon enough I was digging around in my pack for the small billy which held the tiny Rocket stove and a sachet of soup mix.

I sat down in the lee of a small crest in the slope, up against a rock, while the little stove purred along inside the cocoon of its aluminium windshield. From my comfy alcove I took in and savoured the whole moment while slowly chewing over my OSM bar and gazing out into the magic of that late afternoon colour change. Internally, I slowed right down.

Exquisite … enchanted … captivated.

I felt wonderfully at home there, and so I lingered.

Another classic alpine day out close to home. There is definitely a pattern emerging for what appeals to me (especially after reading Chapter 6). What made it memorable?

Was it the early morning crispness and being up to greet the start of a new day? Or was it the hard work and sweat of the climb with the reward of the snowgrass tops again? Perhaps the eerie whiteout of the rising mist, culminating in the revelation of sparkling country breaking through on the other side of the ridge. Maybe, too, that special lift of seeing animals in the wild and the stalk well executed. The shot — good and true; thumping home. Was it the sense of respect for the old nanny in her homelands perhaps? Was it the sense of physical strength in my body as I cleaned up the grunt back to the ridgeline in one pitch? The mountain solitudes? Or could it have been the absolute connectedness I felt as I slowed right down, lingering into the late evening glow in that alpine heaven, before slowly unkinking myself and dropping down through the beech in the half-light at the close of day?

It has to be *all* of the above.

Chapter 9

Simon Buschl — pre-roar on magic tops

An early breakfast and a quick examination through the binoculars to confirm that at least one of the big stags was still there was all that was needed to get us going. We moved around the head of the basin just below the main ridge. No doubt the others we had spotted the day before would also be somewhere nearby, so we kept our eyes out for any deer that might spook the big ones. As we made our way round past some small tarns we noticed there was an incredible amount of deer sign. Unfortunately, we can't have had our eyes peeled on the right spots, because as we approached the head of the basin we disturbed two more stags and a hind that were about 150 metres away.

They ran straight in the direction of the big ones, picking them up as they galloped downhill through a gut and heading straight towards the bush. From this distance we were sure one of the stags would've reached the 12-point mark, with nice spread and length. Unfortunately, we hadn't got close enough to get the shot we wanted and they entered the bush untouched.

We had lost.

This time!

When I heard of this 18 year old and his exploits as a hunter I was immediately transported back to my younger days. Simon Buschl lived to hunt, as I once had. Here was a fellow constantly away in the hills, with his rifle, exploring and fuelling a passion for the outdoors — and all the while living from weekend to weekend to get out and do it all over again.

That youthful vigour, as well as the sheer experience and local knowledge that you build up, gives you an amazing edge when hunting. You're fit from regular trips and the keenness gives you a certain drive to push the boundaries somewhat; staying out later, getting up earlier, investigating and roaming into places that more cautious or less eager hunters might not go. Sometimes, as you build experience, you roam into country that others might not have deemed suitable and lo and behold you end up finding game in all manner of places!

The other factor about Simon that had caught my attention was that as a young hunter of 17 he'd written an excellent article and had it published by one of the leading hunting magazines. This passion for hunting had flowed over into writing stories to share with others. This brought back memories from my early years of putting pen to paper and getting articles into the *New Zealand Outdoor* magazine. Simon also regularly contributes on the fishnhunt online forum as 'Bushman' and his storytelling and increasing skill with animal photography herald a future as a huntsman of note. Look out for his name in the years ahead!

Apart from the connections I felt between Simon and my own emerging years as a hunter/writer, I think that it's great to see such young hunters coming on still. Hunting as an outdoor activity is still attracting youngsters — or perhaps, rather, young men (and women) are still being attracted to hunting!

This encourages me.

Nelson tops — Simon gets into great country for his first article. *Simon Buschl*

Simon is a local Nelson fella, actually the son of a woman I taught back in a past life as a teacher at Waimea College in Nelson. (Meeting the grown young man of a girl who used to sit at a desk in your classroom sure showed up how old in years I've become! At least my heart and mind are still young — well, that's what I think!)

197

Simon's favourite hunting ground is the hinterland around Nelson, particularly on the fringes of Nelson Lakes National Park, and so this story is from that area:

My cousin Mike and I had walked nine hours to get to a bivvy on the bushline. The DOC sign had indicated seven hours, but after the record snowfall and extremely strong winds we'd had in the top of the south, there was a lot of damage to slow us down in the bush. It'd been a bit of a long hike in the January heat, but I quite liked that. Mike's really fit and training up for multi-sport events, so he really pushed me along. I kind of enjoy the physical part of hunting anyway. We'd aimed for this particular piece of high country in the hope of seeing lots of game and we weren't to be disappointed.

On reaching the snowgrass country, I moved to a lookout point and lay down to quickly check the surrounding guts and hollows before darkness set in. Across a small valley down near the bush edge two hinds were spotted moving up from the bush. A few hundred metres ahead there was a stag with his head down, feeding. Later still, another hind and fawn were seen wandering in among the tall native tussocks. After we'd had enough fun watching these deer we moved up a bit higher towards our camp and spotted three more stags of six points or so. But as it was getting dark we were unable to get a good look at the biggest one. These deer fed uphill and we left them in peace to go and get settled into the hut, knowing that indeed we'd arrived into some prime hunting country.

Our basic plan was to get up early as the light got into the sky and head up the hill for a few minutes and get into a position to look over all the country nearby. We'd check out where the animals were and if there was nothing about or if they were settling down in one area, we'd go back to the bivvy and have a big cook-up for breakfast. We couldn't locate the group of five from the evening before but we did spot four large stags about 800 metres from the bush edge, and we decided to go after these big ones another day. Because it was January, the days were long and we had plenty of hunting time, so an extended breakfast back at the hut seemed a good idea.

[I asked Simon if he carried lightweight food to the tops. It seems that, having an older cousin who was into fitness training, combined with Simon being in good shape from sport and hunting, altogether meant that weight considerations were not much of an issue to these fit guys. Also it didn't matter if cans of spaghetti and peaches came along as easy treats either. Besides, the weight training on the way in meant the guys were fitter for lugging out heavy packs bursting with meat!]

We spent two glorious days up on those tops in just the best weather. The cloudless days meant we got great views out towards Murchison as well as back towards Nelson. We'd travel along the main ridges and look into great basins on every side, and the travelling was all pretty easy. Sometimes we'd have a sleep out on the tops in the middle of the day or just sit around in T-shirts and soak up the sun. We'd yak about all sorts of things — about 'girls', hunting and other hard-case stuff — it was all real casual. (Certainly not like the nasty trip Mike and I did later onto the tops above Rapid Creek, on the West Coast. On that trip the rain was persistent and the spur we travelled up wasn't as clear as we'd hoped. The old cullers'

199

trail was so overgrown we got really soaked pushing through the vegetation. Any hope that it would be better on the tops was quickly squashed when we had to wade through waist-high snowgrass that was drenched in water and visibility was next to nothing. Thoroughly soaked, we had hoped that it would turn out better the next day, but it just continued raining. At one point the rain eased off, but this didn't provide any better visibility, so we packed up and sloshed back to civilization.)

We had some special moments during our two days on those Nelson tops, especially as we were seeing plenty of game, mostly deer. We had culled out some goats that seemed out of place way up high in these basins and the odd chamois gave us some challenges when trying to stalk in close. We also bumped into a lone tramper coming off the main ridge, in the middle of nowhere. It was a total surprise to see another person there and he stuck out like 'dogs' balls' against the light-coloured snowgrass.

One highlight was coming upon two reasonable stags out in the lower regions of a nicely grassed basin. We had planned to shoot some venison later, down in the valley floor, on the homeward journey and so had been all packed up and heading out when we came across these two. They seemed real handy, though, and there was the added opportunity of a photo.

The deer were about 300 metres away and both carried reasonable velvet heads, as far as Nelson antlers go. We'd agreed the day before that the big stag we were after then was going to be Mike's, but because these were smaller heads it was to be my shot, as I hadn't really got a good stag yet. Because I wasn't confident at that range we opted for getting in closer. It was a bit of a dodgy stalk because for most of it we were out in full view. The smaller stag seemed to be uncomfortable and numerous times looked directly in our direction and sometimes for up to five minutes, which feels like forever in that situation. We managed to cut the distance down to around 200 metres. Once in position I tried to get a photo of the animals with the little zoom cranked out to full and managed a pretty good picture of the stags in the open. They were a bit alarmed at this stage, so I got busy to take the first shot and lined up on the biggest animal through the Burris scope. When all was pretty steady I squeezed off a shot from the .25-06. I use 117-grain bullets and the animal was hit well but didn't go down, so Mike let off a shot from his .308, which also hit the target. The stag wasn't well but kept going towards the bush edge with us following it up with a small volley. It was turning into a bit of a disaster. We raced ahead and right at the bush edge we finally managed to finish the job off.

The other stag had also taken off towards the bush during all this shooting, but as we walked down towards the dead beast we caught his movement. This stag seemed to be hanging around looking for his missing mate and was a bit mixed up as to where to go. I grabbed for my camera and in the next few moments managed six really good photos of the eight-pointer at close range, up against the bush background. I love those shots because they were my first real sharp photos of a live wild animal. It was pretty special being in that close.

[I managed to catch a set of images taken by Simon in some other Nelson country at an even closer range; you can clearly see the cap of his hunting buddy with a velvet stag standing in the

same frame. In fact, Simon also managed some mpeg footage of the stag at around 10 metres. The animal was barking and thumping his foot, wondering what the heck the two objects were crouched in among the rocks and tussock! The photo would make great advertising material for the benefits of the Stoney Creek camo gear the two hunters were wearing at the time. The fact that the breeze was in their favour points to how close you can get if the animal's prime sense of smell isn't alerted. Mind you, that stag wouldn't have been so curious if the mystery objects had a noisy rotor wing whirling as well!]

The eight-pointer hung around wondering where his mate was. *Simon Buschl*

After those few special photos we let that stag go and went over to cut up the dead one. By the time we'd cut off the legs and grabbed the backsteaks we'd decided to stay at the hut again. I also grabbed the eight-point velvety antlers as a memento. We carried all this back to our packs and somehow shoved it all in before heading for the bivvy. We had decided to do all the boning out back there and it sure was a grovel to the hut.

It was a long and tiring walk out the next day but we made the car park in fairly good time as most of the trip was downhill. We relieved ourselves of our heavy packs and were grateful for being back, but at the same time we wished we could have stayed a few more nights back there on the tops. That's a feeling I think all of us hunters have experienced before.

Heading home with a full pack on the long trek out. *Simon Buschl*

About a month later we heard through the grapevine that a helicopter had buzzed over that very same area and got approximately 40 deer off the tops. Who knows, maybe those bigger stags knew what to do and escaped the chopper. Perhaps that's wishful thinking — but the only way to tell is to go back!

For Simon, the main memory of that trip was about being out there on the tops, with several days of perfect weather, great views and with plenty of wild animals, which they were able to stalk in close to.

'I think what was special from that hunt was that I caught the excitement off my cousin Michael for hunting on the tops.'

Michael is older than Simon, but he had given him that new edge to the hunting he had already done with his family, especially with his father.

It was Simon's dad, Laurence, who had taken Simon along on fishing and hunting trips from an early age. Simon got the chance to fire a shot out of his father's 7mm-08 when he was just eight years old (by his account, Laurence reckons the recoil moved the young Simon backwards across the shooting mound!). There was a close group of family friends comprising Simon's uncle, Gerald, and his cousin, Mike, among others, who would often gather at the family bach at Lake Rotoiti. They would go out bunny shooting in the evenings, down on the Teetotal Flats and it was here, while bush stalking some gullies with his dad, that Simon shot his first deer at age 13.

During long weekend stays, the family would also head off on fishing forays, deeper into the national park. They often combined trout fishing during the day with an evening or morning stalk along the bush fringes of the Travers or Sabine valleys. This set the young Simon up well for the outdoor life, and while at high school his parents were happy to let Simon and his mate, Johnny Christie, get away on weekend hunts into the local foothills behind Richmond.

Spending time in the outdoors is a family affair — Simon at left. *Simon Buschl*

At that stage Simon was just 14 and had to be dropped at the Hackett road-end by one or other parent. Arrangements would be made for a pick-up time and the boys would stride out for some adventuring, mostly spending their time bush stalking and learning where to find animals.

205

Simon's early art work — an impression of a stag he'd like to meet one day! *Simon Buschl*

'I don't mind bush stalking,' says Simon, and yet by the time of his hunt on the tops with Mike his horizons had extended and new country was calling. The confidence gained during that trip has also helped Simon in regularly getting onto game. In 2010 as an 18 year old he has already guided his mates and some younger aspiring hunters onto their first chamois kills. Now, Simon is keen to get as many photos as he can on trips and managed to buy a good-quality 'point and shoot' camera with an optical zoom lens, so that he can add to his photo library.

Naturally, he's had to first get his hunting gear sorted, as this is still his prime motive for being out on the hill; especially because venison is now pretty much expected for BBQs at his dad's squash club. The Tikka rifle was Simon's first main expense, as he moved up from his dad's weapon and over the last few years he's acquired the Stoney Creek 100 Litre Hauler, day pack and gaiters, as well as a Black Stag sleeping bag. He's gradually building his kit and if you follow the signs to his hunters' den out the back of his parents' place, you can come across this gear ready to go, along with the trail bike.

What's really noticeable, though, is that Simon is still keen to hunt with his father and they manage some trips each year. I'm guessing Simon gets to carry a good portion of the loads because his strong number eight frame is in fine physical shape, coming in just under six foot and weighing in at around 83 kilos. Simon, no doubt, can walk the legs off his dad, but he did concede to me that Laurence is still probably the better shot, especially lying prone — but for how long?

I felt a classic hunting moment from Simon should be shared in this book to help round out the different generations of New Zealand hunters I've been trying to represent. I wanted to

207

be sure that those elements of the hunt that make for classic memories from my era were still there for younger hunters as well. Why were they still drawn to hunting? What was it that made a great hunting experience for this generation of young men?

And does the future look promising for New Zealanders in the generations to come?

[In 2011, Simon joined me on a hunt into Fiordland. He proved himself a natural and gifted spotter of game. He has developed very good bush sense and a keen interest in landforms and wildlife — reinforcing to me the tremendous talent in New Zealand of such young people who are becoming passionate about hunting and the outdoors.]

Chapter 10

Jessica McLees — at home with the rifle

I was mindful from the beginning of setting to writing this book that I could not finish without considering how generations of women have also been drawn to hunting and the skills that go with adventuring in the outdoors. There are many female hunters in the ranks who have arrived from a variety of pathways into what some have considered a male bastion. Some are graduates of HUNTS programmes; some are outdoor pursuit enthusiasts who have taken up the rifle as part of their responsibilities to the proper management of our game animals or for a better sense of connection to their food.

Many others, however, have arrived at a love for hunting from engaging with their parents' adventures out on the hills. Much credit should be given to those fathers and mothers who have put a pack on their children's back and hiked them off into the hills on hunts to gather wild meat. Or perhaps some have come into hunting as part of a rural lifestyle, where parents have always been all-inclusive in raising their children to the matter-of-fact ways of the animal kingdom and our place in the food chain, as well as our roles as stewards of the land and the source or gathering places of our foods. In fact, in many cases hunting forms part of the whole configuration of rural life.

Jessica McLees is 16. She grew up on a farm in Southland and her parents run Dunluce Station, which is now in its third generation of the family, since the Irish immigrant Henry McLees started the farm in 1893. Dunluce is bounded on one side by Sunnyside Station in Western Southland and lies off the same road-end as Glendearg, a place of which I have many happy memories of farm life back in the 1970s.

A young Jessica with the results of another evening hunt on the farm. *Mike McLees*

Jessica can look out from the house windows towards Diggers Hill where Ken Pearce and I used to hunt and she could go down to the farm boundary, cross the Waiau River and be right in among the same bushlands and clearings of the hunting country mentioned in the next chapter.

210

Her father, Mike McLees, runs the 538-hectare property and has taught Jessica how to hunt and to use a firearm. He was with her on the night of her memorable hunt — the day she shot her first deer, in 2007, at age 13.

Jessica nowadays on Dunluce Station. Diggers Hill and the bushlands beyond. *Mike McLees*

They'd been out the evening before with Brian Moroney-Pearson who worked for the Gow family on Belmont Station, just up the main road a bit. He had been seeing deer out on a turnip paddock next to the bush at all times of the day. They'd gone down the lane on the four-wheeler and stopped at a shelterbelt where they could see the paddock. There were several deer out so the three had carried on down the lane past them and parked behind the broom along the edge of the

211

creek. Evidently, the deer were used to the noise of farm bikes and Brian had said they quite often stayed there when he went past — and sure enough they did.

There was a hind and weaner on the edge of the paddock next to the bush, and Brian had said Jessica should shoot the weaner. Sneaking forward, they'd got to the fence so that Jessica had something to rest on. The deer were about 100 metres out and Jessica had been a bit nervous about shooting but fired anyway. The bullet fell short and the weaner jumped back, but the group just moved further up the paddock.

At Brian's suggestion they moved over into a hollow that ran along the edge of the paddock and they sat and waited to let things calm down a bit. A spiker came out into the paddock and this was to be Jessica's next target. Unfortunately, a clear shot didn't present itself and the light was fading and making it harder to see the deer against the background of the bush. They were still feeding and playing about when something bigger came out and herded them all back into the bush. They'd seen nine deer that night and so decided to return the following evening. That was to turn out more successfully.

Jessica takes up the story.

It was a good day and as the evening approached we went off down the road on the farm bike and along to the boundary of Belmont Station. It was getting onto dark and there was a pretty stiff breeze blowing across the paddock, but there wasn't anything out as there had been the night before. We went out into the paddock and sat in the shelter of a wee hollow. We would have a look every five minutes or so, hoping that the animals would move out from the bush. Nothing much was happening and we were starting to lose the light, so in the end Dad and Brian thought we would call it a day.

Brian stood up but then suddenly dropped back down again.

There were deer out further up the paddock! They had come out but must have been hidden by a bit of a rise. We all checked them over and Dad decided I should try to take the spiker, so we crawled out to a rise in the paddock just off to our left, where we could get a better view. The deer were just feeding like the previous evening and I could pick the stag out with the naked eye but was having a bit of trouble seeing it through the scope from a sitting position. My heart was throbbing and even using my knees as a rest I was waving about too much, especially with the wind.

Brian told me to just take my time, but then the spiker just plonked himself down for a rest.

Now that we knew he wasn't going anywhere I had a bit more time to get a good rest and line him up in the scope. It was real poor light but when I put the scope on the spiker I could see his head and parts of him but not all of his body. I was able to guess where the biggest part of the body was in the grass. I'm not really a very good shot so I aimed up on the general area of this and after a long time trying to get steady, I took the shot.

Well, the deer just tipped over and I couldn't believe I'd shot it!

The other deer that were with him just stood there looking around.

We started walking over to the spiker and then we could see him trying to get up so we broke into a run. When we were over

213

halfway to him the other deer finally trotted away and when we got to the stag Dad rushed in and cut his throat.

[I asked Jessica if she had any squeamish moments with this, but being a farm girl she'd been around while Mike had slaughtered sheep for farm meat. The rabbits or hares she'd shot previously had been in varying states of dismemberment as well, so she was used to the realities of such things.]

Dad reckoned that the shot was just over 100 metres and the .243 had hit him in the middle of the back, breaking his spine. He wasn't going anywhere. I was pretty happy to have hit it because I'd missed a couple of deer before. I'm not sure why I'd been missing them as they're pretty big targets and I do all right on rabbits with the .22 whenever I go out spotlighting or just go out for a walk around the paddocks in the evening.

Well, the others all congratulated me and took photos and then Dad gutted it while Brian got the bike and we loaded it on and headed home in the dark. Hanging up, he weighed 94 kilos. Dad reckoned it was a not a bad effort for my first deer, in what were tough conditions. I think he was pretty pleased, as he's still got the photos on his computer screen!

I think the really good part about shooting my first deer was that I was out with Dad.

I've never felt that it's anything different that I'm doing, even though the other Year 12 girls at my high school aren't into hunting.

Jessica plans to go on from Southland Girls to study farm management and agriculture at Lincoln University. When I asked her if she'd want to hunt when she's at university she said,

'Sure', and so I told her about the tahr and chamois living in the mountains not too distant inland. There's a great fraternity of young hunters living at those Canterbury universities, and plenty of great stories appear on the fishnhunt online forum coming out of this next generation of ardent hunters.

Certainly, Jessica is keen to explore new country when she finishes her high school years and moves away from Southland. For now, her interest in the family land brings her keenly home each weekend from boarding in Invercargill.

Most weekends she manages to fill up with activity. She loves getting outside and loves seeing wild animals poking around. The excitement and classic challenge of getting that first deer is matched with the adventure of taking her first deer all on her own. This deer was taken early one morning while her parents were still in bed and before heading off to local netball games in the afternoon. She'd wanted to be on the hill at first light on that misty morning and had gotten up really early only to be greeted by light drizzle. Many others might have given it away because of the weather but 'The weather didn't bother me,' she says.

Wandering out the door before first light, in her Swanndri oilskin vest and gumboots, she'd headed up the fenceline on the hill block and cut around towards a smaller knob on the skyline. No fancy Gore-Tex jacket for the rain, no expensive boots for grip in the mud; just standard farm gear and a beanie.

Two wild deer were spotted near the top of the hill tracking along the fenceline, probably making their way back to the bush and scrub cover. Jess had crouched down to let them quieten down a bit and to see what they were going to do. One animal

215

calmed and moved off the fenceline a little and in beside some scrub. Jessica had coolly removed one gumboot to use as a rest for the rifle she was carrying, and settling the crosshairs on the chest, had let off a shot. She's pretty sure the first shot missed as the animal didn't go down but for some reason didn't charge off either; perhaps it was unsure where the shot had come from. The second quick shot connected and she could see it was definitely hit. But it wasn't going down and Jessica wanted it dead for sure so proceeded to empty the magazine. This did the job and she had her second deer for that year — all by herself.

Fortunately, she'd carried the walkie-talkie up the hill with her, so it was a simple matter to call in and wake Dad up. Before long he arrived at the top of the hill with the truck and they both began the job of getting the animal over to it and back down to the shed for butchering. Mike reckons she's gonna have to do the whole job with her next deer, as this is all part of the process of learning everything that goes with the hunting and shooting end of things.

Nowadays Jessica is using Mike's .308 and he seems to be relegated to the .243 or the older .308, but he's happy to have her out on hunts together and pleased that her skills are improving. She likes hunting because she says it's a good skill to know about and good for exercise as well. She states in a matter of fact way that she doesn't see any difference between girls or guys going hunting.

So far, though, her hunts have been confined to the local farmlands and that of neighbouring properties, but there's a good range of both open scrub and bush country for Jessica to build her stalking and shooting skills. She's also been out after pigs and even has a couple of stories published in *Morepork* magazine, with one article relating her first pig hunting trip up on Tower Peak Station in the nearby Takitimu Mountains.

'As a matter of fact I do hunt like a girl!' — a successful one at that. *Mike McLees*

So far she's developed some other outdoor skills, too, having participated in an outdoor education tramp organized through the school. These skills will come quickly to a girl who is used to farm life. She's no stranger to having to deal with the weather and working outdoors because helping Mum and Dad with the

217

farm chores builds that kind of hardiness — farm work doesn't wait for sunny warm days!

I asked Jess if she had a $500 voucher to spend on hunting gear, what she would go and get. She struck me as a very content young woman and simply said she'd probably buy a couple more items of Ridgeline clothing because she's growing out of the ones she's got now! (Perhaps a knife, too, as her present wee pocket knife may not be enough for dealing to a bigger animal in future.) She's fully satisfied with what she has and is happy with just 'mucking around' home on the farm or out with her own working dogs, Bess, May and Smudge.

All in all I reckon Jessica is developing as a good hunter, much like those others I remember being introduced to as a 'townie' when I made my first visit to these farmlands back in the early 1970s. It was the good life of the land and the familiarity with wild animals and their habits that these rural people learnt there on the hinterland of the bush country. And the shooting skills learned in such places are a great foundation for any hunts that may follow in bigger country.

Without doubt, the farm life that Jessica is privileged to enjoy is one foundation that promises much for another generation of hunters coming on. The other firm foundation, though, is that fathers and mothers are still encouraging their children into hunting activities. It's a real tribute to Mike and Lynette McLees that Jessica has developed to the stage where, as a 16-year-old woman, she can wake up early, gather up her gear and head out into the pre-dawn with rifle in hand and with the promise of hunting adventures to be had.

You go, girl!

Chapter 11

Bushland roars

It was definitely crisp as Ken and I eased out into the darkness.

Moments before, the alarm had gone off in the wee shed that we had spent the night in. Ken reached up and grabbed the cord above his head and ignited the one central bright light.

It was a bit of a wake-up shock having the alarming jolt of both ringing clock and that blaring light — but it certainly did the trick!

We were up and into our gear without any words being spoken. Boots on, pack frames all ready and rifles grabbed with one more check that nothing was up the spout before closing the bolt and easing out the door.

Stars were everywhere and with no streetlights back there off the Blackmount-Monowai road it was just sublime in that inky pre-dawn darkness.

Crunching across the gravel, we headed for the three-wheeler parked along with the decades-old jumble of assorted farm equipment that lay among the brewing smells of disused oil, spilt diesel, sacking, old rags and years of dust and tracked mud. I climbed aboard behind Ken and we jolted out of the shed and into the contrasts of chill, pure-smelling air and poorly muffled piston revs.

I was nestled up behind Ken and we slowly motored past the Glendearg homestead before opening up the throttle and striking out towards the upper paddock and the outline of Diggers Hill. The cold swirled around and I kept slipping in behind Ken, not minding to look ahead so much and gathering as much protection as possible from the wind chill beating against us as we sped towards the river. My hands were cold even though they were tucked into the small of Ken's back, and I'm sure his were much worse. Several gates later we were parking the bike into the edge of the bush track that led down to the river.

The beaten up old tin boat was manhandled out from under the tree, turned over and dragged down to the Waiau River with gear placed inside. The boat was made ready with that certain amount of precision from Ken's many forays into this country in Western Southland. I'd come down to this farm a couple of times now since hooking up with Ken when I was in my mid teens and this was to be my first roar trip over the river and into the bushlands. Our love of hunting had been the first connection for a friendship that was to go on and span all of our adult life thus far.

With me in the stern, Ken shoved off with his oar and with a few heavy strokes ferry-glided out into the current of the pool we were crossing. A couple of alignment strokes made the crossing easy and in a few moments I was clambering awkwardly out of the boat in the shallows of the far bank, trying to avoid getting my feet wet. We dragged the boat up onto the rock ledges, stretched out the old rope and wrapped it around a handy tree before picking up our gear and setting a course in the gloom along the river's edge.

Ken knew this country intimately, having grown up at Glendearg and hunting across the river for longer than he could remember. He'd gotten so good at it that he would stand at the lounge window of his parents' home and gaze out with binoculars at the clearings on Diggers Hill at the end of the day. If he spotted an animal he'd be off before tea, down across the paddock, over the river and up onto those bush clearings to shoot it just on dusk, before hauling it down through the bush and reversing the whole process in the darkness.

Soon enough Ken turned off the river and we slipped into the darkness of the undergrowth, and the cover of the bush closed around us like a shroud. We didn't use a torch and there were no headlamps in those days. We just had that bush 'sense' and found our way in the darkness as we climbed up through the trees, with the only sounds being that of our heavy breathing and the crunching underfoot. I could also feel my heart rate increasing as we took to the work of gaining altitude, all the while angling towards the big face where we hoped to catch animals at first light, retreating from the grass towards the bush.

As we neared the face we could see the glow in the eastern sky and knew we'd judged our timing well. With all things in order we stopped to gauge the wind, watching the mist of our warm breaths drift away into the bush. Everything was looking good and as the light grew we checked our riflescopes and eased a round each into the breech of our rifles. In those days Ken was using a Browning Bar semi-auto in .308 calibre, which he kept on safety. He was a deadly shot with this set-up. I carried the 7x57 BSA Hunter on half-cock and was a one-shot-kill man myself in those days — in open country!

It's really cold in those moments after the dawn and before the sun gets onto the horizon; this morning was shaping up to be a real cold one as we scanned the face in front of us from the protective cover of the bush edge. Frost was heavy on the grass and we strained to make out any shapes standing stark against the whiteness of the slopes.

But nothing was about and so we rustled ourselves and walked out into the dawn, as much to pick up some warmth from movement as to shift into new views around the face. Angling across the grass, we came towards the lip of another gully and with heart pounding in my head and rifle at the ready we eased into new views. Ken lifted his rifle and peered through his scope in the direction of a shape down among some manuka and that accelerated the edgy excitement building in me ... but it was just a shape; nothing.

We carried on, sidling around and up to look into more unseen terrain. The night sky was almost gone now, with the last stars turning their lights off as it were and the new day was upon us as we scanned every possible feed area on the big face. Occasionally, we'd notice fresh sign in the grass and could see where animals had tracked off through the frosted cover. They'd been about but it looked like they'd moved into the bush earlier than we had anticipated or had just been ahead of us while we'd been back at the first viewing spot lower down on the bush edge.

We had hoped to catch a roaring stag, but Ken assured me they were probably deeper back into the bush where gullies thick with undergrowth and bog wallow holes were the attraction for their mating season.

With this in mind we climbed up to the ridgeline spur and pushed back into the beech.

The whole game changed now and we moved along 20 or so metres apart, scanning ahead, constantly on alert as we bush stalked along this highway from the open country to the bushlands. Sign was drizzled about in places and animals had definitely been moving along this ridge. At first this tense bush stalking is exciting as it's ever likely that an animal will materialize in front of you somewhere. Silently, you sneak along and curse yourself when you disturb the natural sounds and motions of the bush with the breaking of a twig underfoot or a sudden movement.

After a time of expectant concentration, though, I lose the excitement of such stalking and seem to give more attention to making sure I'm keeping about the same pace through the bush as Ken so that we stay in contact visually.

And then … without warning … there's the movement — a deer.

A hind and yearling materialize among the verticals of tree and bush along the ridge, their shapes slipping silently through the forest some 50 metres in front of me, crossing from right to left. My rifle comes up but all I can see is trees. I look again with the naked eye and then back through the scope, trying desperately to isolate the deer from the forest. They stop and then for a brief moment I try to focus in on them through the clutter in the scope picture. No clear shot. Damn. Then they move again and I follow them … shoot, no wait … and then …

They're gone.

Damn it!

Just as suddenly as they came into view in that silent world of trees they had disappeared, the forest closing around, obliterating their form.

Ken joins me. He'd seen them, too, just as they'd moved up onto the ridge where I was. He wondered why I hadn't fired. I wondered why I hadn't fired! Too slow; too indecisive it seems. In the world of the bushlands Ken reckons you've got to get the lead into the air if you're going to be successful! Waiting for a nice clear view is just not going to do it and I spend the next few hundred metres of stalking chastising myself on this very point before getting back into the business of the hunt.

Eventually, though, the concentration of peering through the wood and listening intently to my footfalls get to me again and I head over to Ken to call a rest stop. Together we search around for that possie that's just right to plant ourselves down and then we go through the deliberately slow moves of digging out a snack from our daypacks so as to fully savour the treat of a rest in the bush. It is nice to slow right down and to let the mind free of the more intense focus required of it during the hunting hours. Sometimes we chat in low murmurs and at other times we just gaze off into the bush and allow ourselves to become more aware of all the other noises that have been tuned down while stalking. There's the gentle wind in the tree tops and the distant quiet of space all the way out to faraway mountains, and the longer I listen the more birdlife I seem to hear, too. I know these things have been there all along but it's amazing how a refocus accentuates what you hear.

Soon enough, though, some idle chatter turns to our plan of attack for the remainder of the day. After all, we're here to hunt.

Ken was for heading deeper into the bushlands, taking us further away from this ridge and into the deeply vegetated creek heads. I add my opinion about how that'll extend our homeward trek, but together we're keen to find where the action is for this roaring season. So we bundle ourselves together and change course, moving more briskly, deeper into the hinterland at the back of the Lake Monowai tops.

After a change in the pace I feel more invigorated and once we've gained a bush plateau we spread out once again and settle into a more deliberate stalking mode. Here the terrain is less open and dry than the ridgeline we were on previously and underfoot is swampier, with animal tracks once again becoming more evident. We end up signalling each other through the trees when we spot fresh sign or marks in the mud and the sense of anticipation rises again as our senses pick up animal life. We know we're in the right place.

Suddenly, a moaning roar drifts up from away off to our right. In a flash our eyes are on each other and in that moment we both feel the lift even more, fully charged with the thrill of the hunt once again.

With some discussion we agree the stag is down in some creek head below the plateau, and a check of the wind lets us know we've got the drop on him with both favourable breeze and height. It's all on.

We waited at the edge of the plateau with ears strained,

listening for that sound that quickens every hunter's senses.

Another roar drifts up and with that we're off over the side!

With Ken keeping a quick pace in the direction of the roar we soon find ourselves in thick going. The undergrowth is denser here and we push through, around and over thick ground cover while all the while listening out for further roars to help our direction.

Another roar — louder this time. We lift our pace even more, keen to close the gap as much as possible in case he goes quiet on us. Soon we strike really thick undergrowth around a small stream and the slope eases off. Sign is everywhere and we realize we're getting close now so we pull right back on the pace and shift into stalking mode.

A booming, deep roar ahead bursts my excitement levels right off the scale and we both hunch into a sort of 'super stealth' stance. We know he's ahead in the bogs of this stream.

Suddenly, a great waft of stag stench fills the air on the drifting breeze and Ken and I peer at each other with that all-knowing awareness of what's to come.

Our pace is really cautious now and I check the half-cock of my rifle for the umpteenth time. Stag smell is thick in the air; in fact, the air reeks of it and this stimulates an even more intense reaction in us as we screw our narrowed eyes into such an extreme focus and our muscles into high tensile readiness. We peer further into the thick undergrowth in front of us. We seem to sense animals, and we can 'feel' them sensing us! We can hear seemingly impossible sounds; we can hear silent hooves on ground, animals breathing, ears twitching. It's extremely intense.

We puff breaths to check the drift of our vapour and we try to just morph into foliage as we creep forward, ever so slowly. There's roaring all around us, the forest is one big booming base amplifier, resounding pulses of this most primal of sounds.

Surely the hinds can hear my hammering heart beat, my every strained nerve? Surely they sense us?

Suddenly, the forest bursts into pandemonium. Shapes crash off ahead of us.

In an instant Ken is gone.

He's sprung forward and a shot booms out echoing all around me. Crashing seems to be coming from all directions. Another shot. The noise is everywhere.

I don't know where to look.

And then I see brown forms flashing through the trees to my left as parting undergrowth marks the dash of hooves. My rifle is up but it's all a blur through the trees. No time, no lead in the air. Another shot from Ken — hell — where are they all?

'Finish the stag' is the yell from off to my right, as suddenly a form comes crashing through the trees towards me. Without even registering my rifle comes up and somehow the scope picks the rush of animal flesh and the shot is on its way. With a great cacophony of crashing body mass and muzzle blast the animal stumbles forward and crashes in front of me as yet another hind bounds past to my left. They're everywhere!

And then … they're gone.

The bush goes deadly quiet and the smell of gun smoke, adrenaline and putrid muddy stag fills and suffocates the air. And the smell of warm blood and death is there, too.

I go over to the stag as Ken materializes from my right. I'd

227

never seen anything of him since that first fleeting moment as he dashed forward, rifle coming up. He'd fired several shots before I'd even thought of firing my first, let alone got my bearings on the departing herd of the stag's harem. What a rush!

Walking about the cattle-yard of this stag's lair we took stock of the damage. Ken had killed one hind, slowed another animal with a gut shot, finished it off and then mortally wounded the stag, which I had finished off.

The last few moments had been full on and I needed to let the tight strain ebb from my adrenaline-charged system. The business of death meant we had to cut some throats and this more deliberate task allowed time for my heart rate to come down.

We both stood there taking in all the replays of the last few moments. Ken was grinning, still pumped up, and you could easily see the enjoyment he got from the thrill of the hunt and the shooting. He was extremely good at this. Close quarters, quick shooting, dealing out death in lethal fashion. He's a great bush hunter and a great bush shooter.

Me — I was still in shock at how quickly it all happened. This was a far cry from the more deliberate stalking in alpine country where you spot the animals from kilometres away and navigate your way around ridgelines and gullies to keep out of sight as you close the distance. And the shooting requires marksmanship which is often more like target practice with a steady rest, albeit while often leaning over lumpy rocks on a bit of an angle. But this bush shooting was a whole other business to me.

The animals lay at several spots through the bush and our replays tried to fathom where the animals had been holding and how many there were, but we couldn't really account for the size of the harem. Obviously, there were two hinds in residence and I'd seen at least two others crash off, but we felt there were more. Without doubt, the amount of sign around indicated this stag had a pretty good serving of the local hinds. The stag himself was a typical bush stag of that region and his little dark antlers of eight points would remain behind as we set about the butchering in preparation for our homeward journey.

The task of stripping off legs and boning out meat was deftly handled by Ken whose years of home-kill on the farm showed up my poorer experience in this domain. Practice makes perfect, though, and it was kills like this alongside a more experienced man that served me well in gaining knowledge that is useful still to this day.

We worked side by side and eventually had a great stack of boned-out meat that went into all manner of muslin and plastic bags, inside day packs and oilskin parkas tied around our waist. But then came the inevitable sinking feeling as we sat down and wriggled into our harnesses. The load was enormous! These Southland animals are big deer; we could hardly climb to our feet. We had to assist each other to stand and while bent over, almost double, we looked off into the bush slopes we had to ascend and the reality of it all settled heavily upon our shoulders. The grunt was about to begin.

And a grunt it was.

Great streams of sweat poured off us as we ever so slowly

gained the plateau level in the bush and trudged along with barely any lift in our feet. In fact it was more of a shuffle because the weight was so heavy that one leg was barely sufficient to hold the burden while a step could be taken. At least on the uphill we'd been able to grab a tree as a sort of a handrail and pull ourselves up, boosting any stepping.

This really was the work of bringing home meat and we knew it. On and on we lumbered, learning again the skill of focusing on a tree in front and stumbling to it before re-targeting another goalpost — a mission, one step at a time. Hours went by. We certainly had been deep in the bushlands and now we had to struggle our way back out.

Finally, we came to the uphill pitch that would bring us up to the ridgeline of Diggers Hill. This was our goal, for we knew it was all downhill from there and with renewed energy (of sorts) we struggled up under the increasing deadweight of our loads atop sore shoulders. We were resting for five and walking for five and slowly by this method we gained the ridgeline. Daylight was almost gone.

We'd had a long day of it by now but the downhill and fading light spurred us on.

The scramble down through the bush is best left as an account of pain and there's no describing the agony of it. Slipping and sliding, swinging off trees and shoulders burning, cut with every jolt of the descent and all the while a growing ache in the knees. The forest got darker and darker and even with that natural night vision the trees still began to scrape and every hazard underfoot began to conspire to upset our surge as we bashed downhill on a direct line for the river.

230

We got there, however. Once on the riverbank, though, any relief from the flat going was short lived, as now the weight of meat really sliced into our weary shoulders.

Great fortitude of an extending capacity was building in my mental tank and I now appreciate how this has come to serve me well over the years. Every hunter has to get these reserves from somewhere. There's no short cut to hardiness and resilience and this was my learning ground.

A stag on the edge of the bushlands. *Steve Gibbons*

Boy — was I glad to make that boat. In the pitch-black darkness we'd had to drop our loads and scout around somewhat to make out the exact area we'd crossed. In time we honed in on the tinnie and after jointly heaving our heavy loads into the boat we launched off for the homeward shore.

There's something special about beginning and ending a successful day's hunt in the hours of darkness and feelings of hard-won pride settled over both of us as we chugged across the paddock on the three-wheeler. We'd left the meat on the pack frames back with the tinnie in the bush and we'd return later with the Land Rover to get it all. For now we were focused on Vera Pearce's farm-size dinner that we knew would be waiting, along with plenty of dessert and the fireside tales we'd have for Jock, retelling our story.

Hard day, exciting day, and new country for me; adrenaline-packed in the depths of the bushlands — a classic hunt.

Chapter 12

Unpacking the hunt

'I hunt for a complex of reasons: to learn about myself and the place I inhabit, to be nourished by the land and participate in its rhythms and to answer a call for which I have no name.'

— T Cerulli

I had wanted to 'hunt down the hunt' as it were, through the eras of each of the hunters represented in these pages. I was looking for common themes emerging from their stories.

What was it about these special memories for the older man, Gordon Max, as he looked back over a lifetime of hunting? What keeps the fire of enthusiasm burning brightly for Zeff Veronese as he strides out still, some 40-plus years after that first trip into the Douglas River. And what about my generation? A generation that had grown up hunting in the really tough years of the 70s, when wild game was scarce because of commercial operations — a generation who now in recent times have been drawn back into the hills, as a bit of a renaissance occurs on the hunting scene in New Zealand.

Then there are those such as Jansen Travis who hunt hard

233

and are still searching for the big stag on public land, that is not a product of animal husbandry. He was introduced to hunting by his father, much like both the younger man Simon Buschl and the teenage Jessica McLees. I wanted to include hunters who were not especially sought out to fit the general direction of this book; instead these were hunters within my sphere of contact and who were just willing to share a story. And most of the hunts that have been written about in these pages are not great epics either, showing that meaningful moments can be had with short jaunts closer to home as well. The key, however, has been about capturing the essence of what makes hunting special for us all.

There were several common threads that I began to pick up from my interviews with these hunters as they shared a classic hunt and as I also discovered in writing down some of my own adventures. The themes that you might have noticed appearing are:

- The value of some sort of a 'first' — a first trip into a new and challenging area, an adventure, or the first of a particular animal shot.
- The important role of some sort of 'father figure' — an older man.
- The importance of seeing animals in the wild.
- That the hunting memory was about so much more than just hunting down, shooting and killing a game animal. There were other aspects that made the hunt memorable, such as being out in the wilds with good mates.

I'd like to spend a few pages 'unpacking' each of these themes because I believe they carry some additional insights and significance for all of us, especially as we look forward to our collective futures.

If we think back to our first trips into new country or out after a new species, or even just shooting our first deer, these all came to us as a challenge. Something we turned into a goal. It was that goal which provided the expectant preparation that we so enjoy and it was that goal that motivated us to venture forth, stepping up to the challenges along the way. Firing a big-calibre rifle for the first time perhaps, overcoming the buck fever as we lined up on our first kill of a wild game animal; or possibly that first trip into challenging country that seemed beyond our capability and was perhaps even intimidating. Can you remember those moments? I can.

When Arthur Lydiard first saw Peter Snell he felt the young runner had some possibilities and that Snell could get there to greatness, if he trained and went after goals. Snell, looking back, comments that 'all we have is what we make'. This is the case in thinking over the hunts covered in this book. All these hunters, myself included, have had to expend effort to make these memories happen. This possibly goes without saying, but often we forget that we have to get out there and stretch some boundaries if we're to achieve and make great memories. This is at the heart of adventuring.

The first news Zeff Veronese received back from the guy who flew in with the food drop was that there were plenty of animals in the Douglas but that the country looked pretty steep. But

235

they still went and put in a big walk to make it happen! Gordon Max wanted to keep stretching out to new terrain and in doing so created a lifelong memory from that trip into wapiti country. Simon and Mike moved out from the comfort of known hunting areas to explore new territory on a pre-roar scouting trip. The reward comes from making effort but some hunters always aim for the easy way and shy away from challenging tests; or they don't dream big enough dreams and so limit themselves and their achievements.

That special moment of a 'first'. Zeff gets his first big game animal after immigrating to New Zealand. *Zeff Veronese*

I think about some of the reasons I have extended my boundaries in the way I hunt or the regions I hunt. To a certain extent these stretches to my comfort cause some pain in one form or another. Not that I'm a masochist, but some people would have trouble understanding making such an effort, especially if they think of hunting as just being a hobby. But pain proves you have done something! Pain tells you that you've done the best you could, you've struggled and pushed some limits and possibly shifted those limits somewhat. Pain certifies your worthy endeavour, in many cases. This certainly happened for me when I first went into Fiordland. The time and effort over the ground versus what I envisioned on the map was a painful lesson for me, but I enjoyed being a conqueror — in the end! I know this is how we felt in South Westland, surviving by our own wits and our choice of gear, toughing it out and to some extent strengthened by difficulty. Perhaps we may fear the tough times but at the same time we yearn to be tested by them.

Poet and author David Whyte says, 'The price of our vitality is the sum of all our fears.'

In setting off to first explore new country and undertake hunting missions we face up to many fears. We become 'over-comers' by our efforts. Our fear of the new country or the intimidation we experience are conquered and we feel more vital, more truly *alive*. (So ask yourself what makes you come alive, and then go do that.)

We need an adventure to live! Adventure is written into the heart of mankind.

Many hunters also get a lot from their adventures out with mates. If you share some hard times as well, such as being cramped in a tent during long bouts of bad weather or slugging it out together with heavy loads of meat and antler, you forge links with that person that are much stronger than those developed while sharing a flat white at the local café. Such intense struggle with our environment and the toughness of hard graft hunting actually serves to unite cobbers — for life.

Gordon Max and Tracy Stratford — lifelong companions. *Gordon Max*

I think about the friendship that grew between Gordon Max and Tracey Stratford. Forged in the tough bush routes they pioneered into the likes of Noisy Creek and the weeks under a tent fly in the dampness of Fiordland, these men became like brothers when in the hills. I heard, too, from Zeff that he and his brother Ennio formed such a bond over all their hunts that

Zeff has never been able to find a hunting mate like him since. And Jansen, Simon and Jessica speak highly of the bond they have with their dads and how they still consider them their best mate.

Hunting also ends up creating some ambition in us — to varying degrees. Jansen pointed this out when he commented that he still wants to shoot the 'big one' — a wild animal and not the product of animal husbandry. He loves competing with the animal on their terms even if he doesn't shoot them. When you want to do something that matters to you, you always want to do it better. If you run for exercise, you want to be able to run for longer, or faster. If you hunt, there are many avenues for going beyond the boundaries of where you are at right now. This desire to improve is part of what drives us to attempting those 'first' things and becomes the inspiration for doing even more. A great hunt, a trophy moment or a classic adventure — all lie in that space wherein further ambition is born.

We need generations of hunters with ambition!

As I think to the future, we must strive to ensure challenging opportunities remain for these hunters. No canned hunts, curtailing 'cheater' technologies while making sure there is opportunity to get into the wild and for the wild to impact upon us. We may need to also minimize the known in some ways, in order to keep that sense of a 'first' and allow some space for hunters to go adventuring. For example, this may mean that we don't provide intensely marked GPS route guides, complete with Google Earth imagery, to take along for the walk. Let's retain wilderness along with the 'sense of the wild' as well.

Thankfully, too, there is still today a drawing that calls from the 'deep time' for young men and women to be out hunting and testing themselves on more real adventures while building those wilder skills, such as how to procure meat from the land. Our apparent civilization and its increasingly captivating consumerism and techno-gadgetry have not yet drafted all the young people into the service of materialism and easy living. There are people like Simon and Jess, getting into hunting and coming to realize more and more that they love it. Such a love for the game animals in our wild places and for developing outdoor lifestyles and hunting skills bode well for our collective futures.

As mentioned earlier, one of the first threads I began to pick up from my interviews with these hunters was the role played by a parent, but especially some sort of father figure — an older man. For Gordon it was his Uncle Laurie and then after his death the older Tracy Stratford took up this position. Zeff latched onto his older brother during their boyhood exploits, and Jansen, Simon and Jess have a special bond formed with their fathers.

If I leave Jessica aside from this discussion for a moment, it seems that young men need that process of time with older men as part of their development. Hunting alongside an older male became that activity which fostered progress into manhood for these guys.

Masculinity is a sort of essence that is passed between men. From my reading, it seems also that adulthood is bestowed by an active intervention and involvement by a man (most especially for sons).

US author Robert Bly notes in *Iron John: A Book about Men*:

> The traditional way of raising sons, which lasted for
> thousands and thousands of years, amounted to fathers
> and sons living in close proximity, while the fathers
> taught the son a trade, perhaps farming or carpentry
> or blacksmithing. From the beginning a father would
> lay the foundations for a young boy's heart and pass on
> to him the essential knowledge and confidence in his
> strength.

Young males need to be surrounded by men, and men that
are providing healthy role models, and doing manly things.
Traditional hunting progressions thrived on these bonds
of older men out with younger men, and often there were
ceremonies of passage or rituals that are to a degree lacking
between the generations now. Perhaps a main reason for going
hunting, then, is to just create that context where men can
be men in some sort of social ritual. The father figures in the
stories of some of these chapters have been out there doing
physical things, living cramped in tents and have sweated while
working on the hills alongside these younger men — and have
taught them to hunt, among other things.

Jansen Travis admired how his father 'hunts hard' and
Jansen had to tough it out on many occasions as a result. Now
he enjoys the physicality of hunting. Striving together and doing
the hard yards has a sort of earthy and honourable feel to it.

In his must-read book for men, *Wild at Heart*, American
author John Eldredge says:

Society at large can't make up its mind about men and hunting. Masculinity seems to have been assaulted and redefined into something more sensitive, safe, manageable and, well, feminine and berates men to some extent for doing manly things. 'Boys will be boys' they sigh. As though if a man were to truly grow up he should forsake wild activity, wilderness and wanderlust and 'settle down' at home!

Simon Buschl enjoyed helping this young hunter to his first stag. *Simon Buschl*

Growing boys want to know that they are tough, they are dangerous, someone to be reckoned with. Likewise we men (read 'big boys') want to know that we are powerful; we must know in our core that we have what it takes and will push through to overcome. (I think that's why we like movies such as *Rambo* and *Braveheart* or *Gladiator*.) To a certain extent hunting allows these deep-felt drives some expression as we tough it out, living rough and battling into the hunting grounds to outwit the target on its own turf ... and as we pull the trigger.

So, the passage of growing into a man's world involves healthy levels of challenge and danger and implicit in this is the affirmation that you or I 'can handle it'. This is where the older man comes into play. They might organize the trip and come along to provide that element of experience. They facilitate the 'stretch' and the growth for the younger man as they hunt together. The older mentor shares the hunt, encouraging the other along (meaning 'to put courage in') and help in engaging that positive sense that the younger man will get through and do all right.

Explore, get dirty, take risks, conquer — you don't have to tell a boy to do these things. This is what boys and men do and it makes us feel alive. I think it's in our genetic code, from the beginning; our design! Hunting lends itself well to these experiences, where we can prove to ourselves we have what it takes. We can stand the trials of route finding in the Fiordland forest or overcoming what nature throws at us by way of intimidating landscapes and weather in South Westland. We can endure the pain while carrying out that big load of meat or rack of antler. We can hack it. There is a strange attraction to this for us men! You want to be the sort of 'greater' hunter, who doesn't find it tough or hurting or even just too hard. You

243

don't want to break, but in order to find that out you have to put yourself to the test and get out there, do strenuous stuff and feel the burn. It's that self-knowledge which we gain from this that is important for us men. I reckon if you asked a lot of hunters what proportion of the best moments in their lives came while out hunting, I think you'd find that it's a pretty high percentage.

I think, too, there is that other manly aspect of being the 'provider' that has a lot of relevance here as well. We need to have passed on to us the skills of collecting food from the wilds. There is a certain rite of passage for a man in securing that first kill, butchering it and then bringing it home to eat. It is wholly desirable that the young man's dad is instrumental in the development towards that stage in life, wherever possible. This intimate connection to natural processes and the ancient DNA of life and death just cannot be substituted by other outdoor pursuits for growing up men. Given these combined values of hunting, we have a tradition which we would not want to give up lightly — at all!

So what is the observation that we must carry through and preserve for the next generation?

We need adventure and challenge for our young men. We need to retain opportunities for the coming generation to experience honest and honourable interactions between senior men and young adults while out hunting and killing. And our 'civilized' society needs to accept that it's healthy for these older men to be out there, putting young men in harm's way on tough outdoor quests. Too much emphasis on making things safe and squeezed down to a more manageable state, or in softening real and worthy outdoor adventuring, is to be avoided as we move into an even more 'PC'-biased society. The masculine soul wastes away in such circumstances.

John Eldredge again:

> Adventure, with its requisite danger and wildness, is a deeply spiritual longing written into the soul of man. The masculine heart needs a place where nothing is prefabricated, modular, non-fat, zip-locked, franchised, online or microwavable. Where there are no deadlines, cell phones, or committee meetings. Where there is room for the soul. Where, finally, the geography around us corresponds to the geography of our heart.

Please interpret correctly what I am saying here, though. I am endorsing the masculine engagement that hunting offers both young men and their older mentors. However, I am not supporting machismo where there is an exaggerated display of masculinity, aggressiveness and perhaps without any sense of emotional connection to the lifestyles of hunting and killing. In fact a testosterone-fuelled approach to hunting is instrumental to what can be wrong with hunting and hunters.

Those other factors of hunting, evident in these classic hunting memories, are the same ingredients that appeal to girls and women, too — such as for Jessica in her story. The parent-daughter bonding through hunting can be just as significant.

Perhaps the reason why so many women are anti-hunting is because they haven't been allowed to join in with the boys in the past. Some wonder if they've been kept out because women have a stricter sense about which deaths are needful and which are no more than gratuitous: for fun or the self-indulgence of some ego-trip. I've commented on this before and we men must be on our guard in this respect.

Hunting father Mike, with Jessica and her younger brother James. *Mike McLees*

Sometimes, though, the reason there aren't as many women hunting is that it's hard to get into hunting if you don't know anyone that hunts, or anyone who will take you hunting. As such, many of our female hunters tend to come from a rural farming background, like Jess, or from a family that actively hunts and is inclusive of both genders. Those from other backgrounds could be more encouraging of female hunters.

At times, though, men just need time to get away and hang

out together, much the same as females need time in their own company. Suffice to say through all this, female hunters are in the ranks for many of the same reasons as males. We jointly contribute to the messages and reputation of our hunting lifestyles, as well as to the heritage we all seek to preserve.

Two mates share the excitement of spotting wild game. *Greig Caigou*

Let's move on to unpacking another element of these classic hunts.

It is possibly no surprise that a theme running through all the stories recounted is that hunting is not just about the tracking down and killing of game. In fact, an overriding joy in these memorable moments has been in seeing wild animals and in being out there connecting with the natural world.

You will have seen emerging through the stories of these

different generations that hunters experience phases during their lives. I covered this in my first book when commenting on how I just wanted to fire a gun and initially was keen to just shoot anything. Then I entered a stage where it was all about counting the numbers killed ... before morphing again, in several ways over the years.

Chamois. I love seeing these animals out on the tops. *Matt Winter*

A study quoted by best-selling US author Ted Kerasote in *Bloodties: Nature, Culture, and the Hunt* reveals that some hunters will move on from these early 'phases' that I've described, to the 'trophy stage' where

hunters believed selectivity of paramount importance, passing up what they considered animals of lesser value.

Evolving into the 'method stage', hunters then invested heavily in equipment and discovered pleasure in 'how' the hunting was done — calling ducks or bugling elk, for instance, or using primitive weapons such as the bow and arrow. In the final 'sportsman stage', the mellowed hunter was satisfied merely to be outside and gave up control of the world through pyrotechnics, accounting, collecting or methodology.

I don't believe the life of a hunter is necessarily shaped by a 'cookie cutter' passing in a linear, sequenced or timed fashion from one phase to another like this describes. Nevertheless, there are personal insights to be gained from such studies in terms of our approach and attitudes to hunting. I also discovered some of these differing and changing attitudes to hunting while enjoying discussions with those featured in this book and as I wrote of my own classic hunting adventures.

There have been other really interesting studies done, too, on the importance of different factors that affect our motivation as hunters and which, in turn, affect the levels of satisfaction gained. In reality there are multiple reasons that come into play to affect hunters' levels of satisfaction, and I saw this as I compared the stories in this book. Gordon Max's desire was to just get into the wapiti country and see the mighty wapiti and hear them bugle. For Zeff it was about magnificent country as well, but his classic memory was of a hunting 'paradise', with animals of all three species in abundance in the Douglas River, when he was there in 1964. For Simon, too, it was about seeing a lot of deer on the hoof out on the tops and getting in close to them. Of course, there are other motivations that come into play than merely the number of animals seen or shot and we've seen that in other chapters.

So what are those things that drive us and impact upon our enjoyment of hunting?

A significant study was undertaken in America by research professor Stephen Kellert on the 'Attitudes and Characteristics of Hunters and Anti-hunters'. When reported in 1978, that study identified approximately 44 per cent of the 3200 sampled hunters as people mainly interested in harvesting meat and they had little interest in the animals themselves or their environments. Kellert termed these 'utilitarian/meat hunters' and mentioned a 'pioneering spirit' among this group, noting their 'special respect ... for resourcefulness, self-reliance and individuality'.

A further 18 per cent of the survey he termed 'nature hunters', with these individuals hunting the most often and knowing the most about wildlife. Their goal was to be more intensely involved in nature, through hunting.

The middle profile Kellert called the 'dominionistic/sport hunter', representing 39 per cent of American hunters. These hunters often lived in cities and strove for mastery over animals, where the hunted animal was valued largely for the opportunities it provided to engage in a sporting activity involving conquest, competition, shooting skill and expressions of prowess. There are those who are concerned that this group has often set the public image for the rest of the hunting community. In America, in spite of efforts by organizations to educate the non-hunting and anti-hunting public about the hunter's role in conserving habitat and species, it can be this group's bloodlust behaviour that the public recalls when they think of hunting.

But what about more recent studies and here in New Zealand?

In the following paragraphs I'll draw quite extensively from a New Zealand paper, co-authored by Amelia Woods and Geoff Kerr for a 'Land Environment and People Research Report' in June 2010, titled *Recreational Game Hunting: Motivations, Satisfactions and Participation*. I recommend you get hold of a copy. This report provides excellent insights from many studies both here and abroad and was conceived in order to help understand the aspirations of recreational game hunters in New Zealand, especially if we are to be gaining greater responsibility for managing hunting on areas of the public estate in future.

According to this report, there are 'achievement-oriented hunters' who are motivated by the attainment of a particular goal, such as harvesting an animal for meat, a trophy or achieving a display of skill. 'Affiliation-oriented' hunters participate in hunting with the primary purpose of fostering personal relationships with friends, family or hunting companions. 'Appreciation-oriented' hunters are motivated by a desire to be outdoors, away from everyday stress, to relax, to get involved with nature or perhaps experience personal solitude.

Overall, though, the motivations are either intrinsic to the hunter or they involve an interaction with animals, such as getting a trophy, taking a shot at a deer, or just the excitement of seeing a deer.

There are claims by some researchers that animal inter-action motives are the most crucial in understanding hunter behaviour. It can be argued that the purely appreciation- or affiliation-based motivations can be achieved by taking part in many other activities, such as back-country tramping or climbing. However, hunter-based motivations involving encounters with animals or taking shots at deer are, in fact, unique to hunting.

Experiencing comradeship and some relaxing time in the 'nearby faraway'. *Greig Caigou*

The main point — and most interesting for me — is that when I cast my non-scientific eye over the findings from many different studies, the 'appreciation' aspects such as 'environment' or 'nature' top out all the research in terms of motivation for actually going hunting.

To quote Woods and Kerr (the italics are mine):

Being in or experiencing nature has been consistently ranked the most important hunter-based motivation, with the social aspect of time with family or hunting companions coming second. The third most important motivation is exiting civilization, followed by solitude, challenge, sport and exercise.

When looking at interactions with animals, it was the excitement factor that is foremost over actually shooting meat or a trophy; though probably the excitement of seeing an animal means that there is an expectation of some greater chance later on of taking an equally exciting shot!

Woods and Kerr:

As with studies conducted abroad, it is apparent that it is not essential for most hunters to kill an animal to have a successful hunt, even for multi-day trips entailing greater investment of time and effort. However, it is to be noted that all these studies confirm that there is a relationship between harvest success and levels of actual satisfaction gained from the hunt.

We may be motivated to go hunting for a variety of reasons, but it's a complex mix of factors that impacts upon whether we are actually satisfied with the hunt. The New Zealand studies demonstrate that seeing animals or their sign scores highest in terms of satisfaction levels and was a key factor common among my discussions with the hunters' memorable moments that are recounted in this book.

Success in seeing game, access conditions and other variables such as hunter congestion are all being researched nowadays because they influence the value of the local hunting experience. What is crucial is that we have the potential to increase such value in future, through improved game-management activities on the public estate.

Seeing a wild bull wapiti at close quarters in wilderness bush is pretty exciting. *Steve Gibbons*

The hunting experience is multi-dimensional and specific to each individual hunter. It is obvious that there is a variety of reasons that affect enjoyment for different hunters. I know also that there can be significant differences affecting levels of satisfaction from trip to trip, just for the same hunter. This depends on the goal for the trip, which can vary from getting away from civilization, through targeting meat or just wanting to have an adventure in new places. What I want from a hunt ultimately shapes *how* I hunt also, and in turn this affects the degree of satisfaction.

The author obtains his meat close to home. *Steve Gibbons*

The learning here, then, is that we hunters need to be clear about what it is we want from our hunting trips. We need to also make some effort to consider what is worthy and honourable in this as we develop our own personal credo. Not all hunters hold to a set of ethics to guide their behaviour in the field.

As an aside, among other interesting conclusions from the study by Woods and Kerr, the following comments resonated with me: 'Whilst much of the popular hunting literature places much emphasis on trophies, collecting a trophy is not a primary motivation for most hunters.'

Along with the retailers and manufacturers of gear, perhaps the marketing forces and role models that drive such literature need to give more attention to this element. There seems to be a lot of strong commercial pressure in today's hunting scene, with catalogues growing thicker every year as they billboard more and more stuff. Combine this with individual ambition and jealously guarded information about 'spot X' or privileged and exclusive access rights and the soul of what makes local hunting special may in fact waste away.

All this discussion serves to reinforce the need to manage sustainable populations of game animals for future generations of New Zealanders. All hunters love seeing game in the forest and on the high tops. These animal populations must be accessible by all who can venture out. They must live in environments that are not contrived, meaning in natural wild places, rather than behind fences or on private reserves, where there is not the same sense of wildness and true animal instincts engaged in the hunt. These are the factors that made for classic memories among the hunters profiled in this book, as well as for me.

In finishing this chapter there is one other delight that I discovered during the time I spent with these older men. This happened to a certain extent as I relived my own trip into the Douglas Valley after Zeff had shared his first trip there, but I felt this most strongly when spending time with Gordon Max, recounting his story from the wapiti country.

Gordon had lent me his slide collection to take home. Here were images from his trip into the Glaisnock with his mates back in 1956 (the year I was born). As I flicked through the mix of both colour and black and white slides, I came to an image taken from a spot high in the head of the Wapiti River. The shot was overlooking Blue Lake that spills out of the basin adjacent to the dividing ridge with the Henderson Burn.

The photo was taken from more or less the same place I have stood upon. I have taken my own photo there — some 50 years later!

A sudden sense of something like 'awe' came over me. Here I had been talking with this much older and now frailer man about those fond memories he had of his hunting in that country and now appreciating that I had stood in those same places just a few months earlier.

There's some romance in this, for want of a better word! To stand where another previous generation has stood, on the thresholds of unknown country. To have ventured in the steps of those who have gone before, who no doubt felt the same weight upon the back and enjoyed the same rock camps and to have laboured down in that thick moss and vines of the rock gardens in the gorge. To have looked upon the descendants of the same wapiti which inhabit those valleys.

I felt the power of 'connection' standing where Gordon took this photo in 1956. *Gordon Max*

In unpacking the hunts I was more vividly awakened to the connections between the generations of hunters and the generations of animals that have moved among these ancient and wild landscapes. What occurred to me is that there is something special in this and how much we need to *treasure* such connections we have with those who have gone before. Perhaps I, too, in due course, may be sharing my videos and images with some younger hunter in 20 years' time. That hunter will come around to hear my stories from these areas and we'll chat and I'll relive those classic hunting adventures, when Murray and I spent time journeying up on those ridgelines. I'll tell of our glorious views and the magic moments with the big bull. I'll share that great mental image, which will still be there, vividly burned into my mind's eye; that great heavy rack

258

of antlers protruding wide from his pack as Murray slogged upwards into the void!

I came to realize that this is just one special spot in the vastnesses of Fiordland and yet representative of memories for both Gordon and me (and perhaps others who have been there, too). This spot is untamed. This spot is ancient. Gordon's generation had been there and is sadly passing on and I, in my generation, have stood there also. I, too, am passing on. We are a vapour. But this place will remain — just as it is.

Free to roam these special places with pack and rifle. *Greig Caigou*

For another generation of hunters must stand in awe at this spot, as the vapour-laden clouds billow by — with unmatched vistas stretching as far as the eye can see in every direction. Those views will be that much more momentously glorious because they have been *earned*, during honourable effort down in the tangled bush and rugged gorges, during the strenuous tasks of getting up to that high place.

259

I thought, too, of the wapiti there. The calves following the old cows over this spot and young bulls following the master bulls, traversing these routes around the catchments of the Glaisnock wilderness area. From one generation to another, that's how they learn to live in these lands. The same trails. For them this is important.

We've all walked among those wild horizons.

This place, and many other special places like it, must remain — just as they are!

Chapter 13

Wilderness matters

'The future can no longer be "What is going to happen?" It is: "What are we going to do?"'

— Henri Bergson

In 2010 the alert from the threat of legitimising heli-hunting rallied hunters around some themes that underpin what we love about hunting in New Zealand, and therefore what we absolutely must preserve!

Heli-hunting is the active herding of wild animals by helicopter, allowing a paying client to shoot the trapped animal from the air or to be dropped into position to intercept and kill the exhausted beast. Recreational hunters, many hunting guides, the non-hunting community and other users of the back-country were set firmly against this business. What has been shown through the debates is that we all value a 'full back-country experience' almost as much as we hunters value the seeing and shooting of game. These elements that go into the mix of a hunting trip include the opportunity to be somewhere beyond the workaday world — out adventuring and meeting challenges, relying on ourselves as we connect with the environment and with the wild animals that live there. We value seeing these animals on the hoof and we value the opportunity to hunt them on their terms. I've mentioned in the previous chapter the other things we value as well, such as being away with mates, living rough and bringing home meat or trophy. These things are all part of the authentic hunting experiences that make up our heritage of hunting in New Zealand. These are at odds with what many have come to see as increasingly threatened by invasions of such commercial interests that take away from that heritage.

As hunters at this time in New Zealand we are bound by the deeds of those who came before us and the expectations of those who come after us. We must appreciate, too, that the hunting tradition and the conservation ethic have unfolded over a long period.

The understanding I have of our distant British history was that all property and wildlife was reserved for the sovereign king, who could designate others that might avail themselves of 'privileges'. The kings' interest in wildlife, land and individual rights was intensely selfish, of course, and typically they kept the good stuff for themselves! Successive kings had ruled in our motherland for so long that the rights of ordinary people had fully disappeared. In the beginning, the penalty for 'commoners' hunting on the king's land was death and until as late as our early history in New Zealand, poachers were being flogged, jailed and fined. The king was still sovereign, maintaining heavy-handed control over the wild animals until the time of the birth of colonial New Zealand.

In Britain, the idea of the common hunter as part of a

conservation movement had hardly sprung up at all and our past was influenced somewhat from these embedded attitudes and historical perspectives. But citizen conservation needs to be given more credence now in modern New Zealand, especially as there are new political forces at work.

Wilderness matters — let's keep it that way. *Greig Caigou*

Take the Fiordland Wapiti Foundation's efforts in that part of the country. The Foundation is doing what is right. They are fulfilling the promises of ethical hunters who have gone before, who made endeavours for the animals and to the land. They established a set of commitments not just to the wapiti, because the FWF has a commitment to a legacy of game animals for future hunters, as well as to those great sodden forest and mountain lands brooding in the chasms of the fiords.

Such a wonderful wilderness area has become my inheritance, along with other pockets of wilder back-country in New Zealand. All of these lands and animal populations are now our heritage by virtue of citizenship and as such we are the ones to manage our public conservation lands! We are the tangata whenua. We are the ones who must say what kind of legacy of wild places we want and we are the ones who must jealously guard the impacts upon that wilderness.

The debates that had emerged about heli-hunting's impacts upon 'natural quiet', for example, highlighted to me how we must preserve wilderness-type experiences. There are already designated 'wilderness zones' that restrict helicopter access and these places have minimal facilities so as to provide opportunity for more strenuous effort. Also, by their nature, these places are harder to get to, and limiting access or making access hard is the best approach for maintaining a wilderness experience. This way, only those who are ready and able will overcome the barriers to get into such places.

Ed Hillary, in *Nothing Venture, Nothing Win*, said:

> There are plenty of tamed wonders for all to goggle at through vehicle windows — we must also retain our wilderness areas, where nature can develop in its own calm way and where only those humans who are prepared to walk and sweat a little qualify to go.

Les Molloy and Craig Potton, in *Our New Zealand Wilderness Heritage*, remark:

> Hunters are inextricably linked to wild domains (as that is where the animals retreat to) and it was hunters, like President Theodore Roosevelt and Aldo Leopold, who

were pre-eminent in the quest for preserving America's diminishing wilderness in that country. These men were both preservationist and conservationist in their approach. Just as the young American nation gave the world the concept of national parks, the idea of legally protecting large areas of wilderness also had its origins in North America and culminated in the passing of its Wilderness Act in 1964. New Zealand's concept of an individual wilderness experience and places called 'wilderness areas' largely stem from this American model.

Heartland wilderness. *Simon Buschl*

We can also allow for many of the advantages of such wilderness areas in other terrain as well. Hunters get beyond the established tracks and often camp away from hut facilities, for example. We seek out places away from others and this is where the invasive and unfettered nature of heli-hunting causes most concern. These flying machines can freely range over all these places as they search out game for clients. No amount of 'real-time tracking' is going to get around the lack of monitoring and effective policing required to control this impact on our skyscape and wilderness values.

Hunters rightly want to retain as much of a natural experience as possible, but one element I'd like to comment on is that we hunters must, in turn, do our part to allow for a natural experience for those that come after us. How often do we ourselves impact upon the natural environment and negatively affect others' experience, or indeed leave traces of our presence in the wild areas we visit?

I recall hunting up past a small knoll in a Westland valley to come across dollops of human crap, each topped with a patch of toilet paper. This was spread about in several places, around what had obviously been a hunter's camp site (as figured out by intentions left in a hut book that I read later). The same occurred when a small party of us camped in the upper Whataroa, at a popular site used by previous parties dropped in by helicopter. Not only were there highly visible toileting deposits but food cans and packaging were also in evidence. Very little effort had been made in tidying up, burying or even in taking any of this out (which would have been very easy if the party were to be flown out, but not even much of a burden if they had been walking out either). My point is that we hunters must do our bit in demonstrating our values for natural experiences and leave no trace of our time in our hunting grounds.

'We've all walked among these same wild horizons.' *Greig Caigou*

Another point here is that we must nurture a hunting ethic capable of sustaining a hunting lifestyle in modern-day, 'politically correct' New Zealand. Society increasingly wants

267

to marginalize hunting from those others who want the back-country lands for play-type recreations. We, on the other hand, want to stay close to the ways of the animal kingdom and the deeper participation with things wild. Wilderness-type experiences matter! These things are good for us and the more we can retain of wild terrain and wild hunting, the better. The better for us and the better for those who come after us. We don't want to be edged out because we carry firearms and kill animals or because our activity doesn't blend well with those that think the back-country is only for trampers, mountain bikers, climbers, kayakers or tourists.

For me, as a hunter, I enjoy the *connectedness* to things natural and natural processes in the back-country. When I head off adventuring I'm keenly after all that stuff that wild places foster, much like any of those other outdoors recreationalists. But when I'm hunting, I'm also engaging with the wild places in a more real interaction that goes back to deep time — that of the hunter and hunted. This is when I believe we actually confront nature's rhythms in the closest of ways. This is also why I can't separate my passion for hunting from my passion for wilderness preservation.

Those settlers that came here found a land with a 'first nation', indigenous people who were hunter-gatherers also. They had a very real understanding and view of how humans were connected to the land and with a whole other appreciation of the standing and ownership of the wildlife. Maori have an ethos of kaitiakitanga: the use of and guardianship of their environments and the gathering places of wild foods. Modern New Zealanders would do well to foster these same attitudes and we hunters need to jealously hold on to these principles and the freedoms we enjoy in the places we kill our food animals.

Heli-hunting, for example, is at odds with what matters in a wilderness experience and in the fundamentals of hunting handed to me by my grandfather, and that's why I'm taking aim at this issue, given the prestige of our hunting heritage.

Does heli-hunting really reflect the sort of aspirations we want to foster in our wild environments for future generations? These activities of tramping, climbing, hunting and the like are hallmarks of the quintessential spirit of adventuring in New Zealand and develop the sorts of individual hardihood that we are well known for throughout the world. We reflect these in our values, actions and iconic heroes, such as Sir Edmund Hillary and Sir Peter Blake. Such a core heritage of adventuring is not reflected well by an activity that displays hunting in a disturbing light and in a way that is not permitted elsewhere in the world. Indeed, the activity is wholly unworthy of what hunters all over the world see as integral to their recreation — the close connections to interacting with nature. In fact heli-hunters are going to great lengths to avoid personal interaction with the wild places and their ecology.

Hunting wild animals in peace and quiet, enjoying our public land in full measure is protected because of the efforts of our pioneering, conservation-minded hunters. I'd like to borrow somewhat from Jim Posewitz, who is the founder of Orion, the Hunters Institute in Montana, and an observer and reputable outdoors commentator. He feels it is time to find true north again as we have been 'drifting off course into a system of wildlife management that advantages commerce, tolerates exclusion and creates again a class system'. We'd better watch ourselves within the New Zealand hunting community lest we head down that same trail.

I believe our public lands have been conserved for many things, not the least of which is the ability for our people to learn and have reinforced certain ethics that are important to our culture. These include caring for the environment and the things that live in it, respect for the history that our people have in this place, sustaining ourselves from the land and leaving a better world for our descendants.

Theodore Roosevelt said:

> It is ... in our power ... to preserve large tracts of wilderness ... and to preserve game ... for ... all lovers of nature, and to give reasonable opportunities for the exercise of the skill of the hunter, whether he is or is not a man of means.

According to one commentator, these words are the thoughts of the greatest wildlife conservationist who ever lived!

In 2010 the heli-hunting debate came at a time when the proposal for a Game Animal Council was also gaining some momentum. New Zealanders were rallying to the front lines, much like they have on other continents.

Here's Jim Posewitz again, speaking about the modern situation in American (but just as pertinent for us):

> The social issues within our hunting culture and humanity's relentless pressure on the wild places of earth

are testing our generation as they have tested no other. For us, the real reward is an enriched abundance of game and a sustained democracy of the hunt. If we can succeed, we will have indeed claimed a real trophy — the big prize — the heritage preserved!

The classic hunting memories recounted in this book, and captured across several generations and in a variety of places in the South Island, have all served to highlight some key elements of our hunting in New Zealand. I want to enhance the prestige of such a heritage of hunting and make a clarion call for conservation of our wild places and the authentic way of a hunter's life that we could easily lose. Let's remain vigilant.

There are a few other considerations I think worthy for hunters to consider in regards to our hunter's way of life. These are more surreptitious threats and we do well to be mindful of them also. I believe the battles for the future of hunting are on two fronts — the external forces seeking to overrun the authentic, fair-chase and wild hunting experience we have inherited, while others seek to marginalize users of firearms in modern society. Then there is this other front that often originates from within our own ranks and which has more to do with our own attitudes. I'm talking about where we start to lose the essence from within — the subtle changes and movements away from what is our New Zealand *way* of hunting.

Cultural anthropologist Richard Nelson wrote that authentic hunting 'brings me into the wild, and brings the wild into me.' In many ways we need to ensure the wildness stays in our hunting!

In the past the further out from a road and the longer you were away from civilization, the wilder your experience was. (I think back to Gordon Max in Chapter 3, being left at the lakeside with his mates and having to live by their own skills for three weeks, with no contact with the outside world.) But it's getting difficult to create such an experience nowadays. Perhaps a law of diminishing returns operates with our modern hunting, reducing that level of commitment and skill to meet a wilderness challenge and reducing the need for self-reliance and resourcefulness.

Another incursion to the more wild crafts of hunting lies perhaps on the technology front. There are subtle and not so subtle changes to the way we hunt because of the technologies available to us these days. I'm not saying we stay as traditionalists and I argued this point in my first book on the 'Why of Hunting', but in some instances these increasingly sophisticated technologies just operate to separate us from nature somewhat and reduce the intensity of our experience with the land. We are lured instead into an experience more focused on our technology and gadget-craft and hunting 'becomes soul-less, just a cold calculating list of mechanical tasks, ending with a kill', as hunter Aaron Meikle puts it.

Aldo Leopold, a respected US expert on game management and who with his friends founded The Wilderness Society, wrote in *A Sand County Almanac*:

> There is a value in any experience that exercises those ethical restraints collectively called 'sportsmanship'. Our tools for the pursuit of wildlife improve faster than we

do, and sportsmanship is a voluntary limitation in the use of those armaments. This is the way of wilderness experiences.

Man alone in the wilderness. *Greig Caigou*

The great thinker Henry Thoreau felt that 'in wildness is the preservation of the world'. He was not just referring to wild places but the more elemental interconnections that exist for all life-forms. Hunters are an integral part of that greater life cycle and rather than separate ourselves from that in our approaches to our hunts we need to immerse ourselves more in these natural rhythms. I think the legacy we can leave should have less to do with tools of the trade (such as high-tech firearms, night optics, spy gear and ... *you fill in the blank*) and perhaps more to do with discovering life up close — both in the animal's kingdom and within ourselves.

For some the technologies available today allow for greater appreciation of wildlife, but for many it's all about gaining overwhelming advantage over the instincts of the animals and at times this can relegate the hunt to a meat-shooting gallery, somewhat akin to a 'cheating' heli-hunt! We have been quick to condemn these cheater hunters who scour the hills by helicopter, herding a beast into a no-win situation before shooting it down, but the technological advantage of a helicopter-assisted hunt is not that much further along the same path of some antics or hunter practices we seem to otherwise accept! This is one of the challenges local hunters need to face up to — and have not. At which point along the continuum will we say to ourselves we've gained an unethical advantage over our game? I count myself in on such decisions as well; having to make these ethical choices as to what is appropriate use of technology, what is good practice or not (whether it is deemed legal or not).

How do we pass that approach on to the next generation of hunters — our children?

The capacity of hunting to affect the hunter's worldview is actually built in to our activity, in my opinion. We participate more in the ebb and flow of life in the wild places where we hunt. We shouldn't invade that space noisily, roughly or brashly. We get immersed in it all. Our approach is up close and personal, as part of the environment and in tune with natural laws, and in tune with natural instincts to some degree, not overwhelming them! Our developing hunters need to be challenged with some ethical considerations about the use of different and emerging technologies because otherwise their hunts can be awful, or mediocre at best. They need to ask themselves about where they draw the line on gaining advantage over what they hunt so that in fact they keep alive the quintessential nature of a *'hunt'* — as opposed to 'scoring' in some shooting game of numbers of kills, ranges or sizes taken.

Are we passing on as much as we can of these more 'elemental' aspects of hunting when we take the next generation out hunting? And what messages are we sending to those that come after us in terms of where to dedicate their energies as a hunter? These are worthy aspects of the hunt to give some consideration to with the next generation, because market forces want us to get more rapt with ever more sophisticated gear and an algorithmic conquering of animal instinct.

We are constantly bombarded with such consumerism and therefore perhaps we need to pass on to the younger generation of hunters some sense of *being* while in the outdoors. By way of example, do we give some credence to our maturing hunters of the notion of time out or solitude — a precious commodity which is difficult to find amid the noise of our frenetic urban societies. We sometimes need to be confronted with an untamed and wilder world to be reminded that man is just a sojourner here. This was how I felt when standing on that ridgeline in the Glaisnock wilderness area, reflecting on an older generation of hunters that had stood and marvelled in the very same place. Sometimes, if you stand long enough looking at those grasslands and ancient rock-faces you'll feel like you've been transported thousands of years back in time. If we rush on cramming our hunting trips full of targets and taking more photos for our Facebook page, we are in danger of the wild experience becoming much less than incidental to just the product of shooting game.

Hunting gives that necessary space to our lives. *Greig Caigou*

How do we get across the simple joys of the freedom in the hills, feeling the flow, travelling at will, simply, on nature's terms. This is why I sometimes prefer *not* to Google Earth an area or to have a blow-by-blow description of how to get into somewhere, which ridge and where the camp sites are. I enjoy finding these out for myself, expanding my skills on the ground, embracing the feelings that go with that — this is an element of the unknown and is at the heart of adventure for me. Remove this by having GPS mark every small detail of a journey and I sense I would lose a lot of that element, which I crave.

The idea of a wilderness experience is very personal, but I think it embodies qualities like remoteness and discovery (and this is why I think I preferred to find the rock camp in the Henderson Burn for myself, to some degree, rather than from some 'join the dots' trip plan such as those that are gaining popularity in trampers' magazines). A successful trip for me nowadays does not necessarily mean having all such variables sorted in advance. I don't act foolishly, but I also choose to embrace the challenges at as many levels as I can. Wilderness survival requires the ability to handle major uncertainties, such as intense weather, route finding and difficult terrain.

Aldo Leopold, in *A Sand County Almanac*, put it this way: 'Wilderness areas are first of all a series of sanctuaries for the primitive arts of wilderness travel.'

Overcoming the challenge of travelling through a hazardous natural environment can develop self-reliance, which is increasingly under threat in our society.

Aat Vervoorn, in *Mountain Solitudes*, says:

> Being able to move in the mountains deftly, lightly, with
> a minimum of damage to oneself and the environment,
> requires much more than skill at walking or navigation;
> it requires knowledge that can only be acquired
> gradually by being in the mountain setting and learning
> to read and respond to its signs and to learn and read
> the signs in yourself. This is 'self-knowledge' as well
> as knowledge of the wilderness environment and the
> two come together in a sense of 'belonging', of feeling
> at home and of being subject to the same processes of
> nature.

Henry David Thoreau, that great conservationist, articulated
the idea that humans are part of nature and that we function
best, as individuals and societies, when we are conscious of that
fact. Hunters must not become apologetic to modern societies
for our hunter instincts and our way of life in the hills and
among wild animals. We can't be marginalized. Instead we
must show new and young hunters the great meshing with
timeless processes — the way the natural world works and that
humans are part of that system, even as predators. We must
show how we participate with nature and the source of our life
and food.

Otherwise, in some ways we can be prone to act like 'hunter-
tourists' in our approach to our trips: looking into new country,
searching around for some trophy to take home to tell in our
story. At times I've been like that, too. But perhaps we should

strive to linger more, slow down, take in and feel. This is hunting, too. The explorer Charlie Douglas wrote: 'Nature's true wonders don't disclose themselves to day-trippers. It [the wilderness] is a place to linger.'

I've read that in our aurally blitzed world we are losing the ability to listen well to the sounds and rhythms of nature around us. We are getting out of touch with what can be a sacred connection and that allows time for deep contemplation. The rush to get into the hills and to hunt or pursue some target is only a part of the meaning of being there anyway! It's well worth the effort during these wilderness journeys to slow down, sit still and open up our senses.

In some ways hunting in the wild is a necessary escape from civilization. Our attention span is being chopped into increasingly shorter intervals due to modern life and that is not good for thinking those deeper thoughts. Dutch Holocaust survivor Corrie ten Boom once said we should 'beware the barrenness of a busy life'. I think that because our lives are so frenetic, we need that healthy time-out in the hills. Hunting, whether for meat, trophy or recreation, gives that space to our lives and such quiet time acts like a cure from what can otherwise become a barren and busy, workaday life.

Therefore, we should be careful not to get so caught up in the dash to fit in a hunting goal that we lose touch with other things of value in matters of the wilderness. This also can be an insidious threat to a fuller hunting experience.

A wilderness-type experience can be gained in a variety of natural landscapes, of course, but to keep the widest opportunities for outdoor recreation, management of some large remote wilderness areas is crucial. The wild lands of the world are continually shrinking, so the opportunities we can offer in New Zealand are of international significance, especially for hunters. Competition for the scarce natural resources of these wild lands will intensify. Recreational hunting will be more vulnerable in future, as more outdoor groups will look to limit the range of different uses in certain areas, particularly as hunting is seen as somewhat incompatible with other recreational activities.

Greig and daughter Emma head off to freely hunt abundant game in wild country ... a heritage to preserve! *Emma Caigou*

So, to sum up:

What I am saying is that, on the one hand, we must value and preserve our wilderness lands because these matter for the future of over-civilized people and for the future of hunting. On the other hand, we must also be mindful to value and preserve the wilder-type 'experiences' of our hunting, wherever it is that you hunt — because these matter too for the future of our *way* of hunting. We must be vigilant in ourselves, to not take on and perhaps even to stave-off some of the incursions that are being made into a few of the time-honoured approaches to our more 'real' and worthy ways of hunting in New Zealand.

And like those founding fathers of this country, we can make conscious efforts to ensure our hunting experience is not relegated again to positions beneath those gained via economic status; where those with more wealth gain 'advantage' over our animals by their choice of equipment or access greater privileges on more and more 'gamekeeper-styled' private blocks.

I'm drawn back again to the comments I made at the end of the previous chapter. I recall those photos taken by Gordon Max from roughly the same position as I myself had stood. I can see the lofty peaks and steep-sided valleys with the great vista out over an alpine lake at the head of Wapiti River. What struck me was how hunters two generations apart have sought out these same wilderness places, had arrived by nature of the terrain and route finding at the same viewing spots and had marvelled at the same glorious wilderness all around. What truly sunk deep into my spirit was that though generation after generation of hunters and animals had been coming here, the mountain scene was unchanged.

Unaltered. Immovable. Indescribable. *Whatungarongaro he tangata, toitu te whenua ... People come and go but the land endures.*

What a pity it would be for future generations if they could not access such hunting or if such mountainscapes were changed. It was as if these places were meant for us hunters to struggle into and then to linger for a time; to take in the panoramas, spy on the wild animals, and connect with both the rugged harshness and severe weather of those environments. Also, at other times, to connect with the glorious beauties of those places while enjoying the thrill of our hunting and shooting heritage.

In this respect it's appropriate I end this chapter with the same words with which I finished my first book.

Let's keep it that way, eh!

Chapter 14

A hunter's creed

Why do I hunt?

It's a lot to think about, and I think about it a lot.

I hunt to acknowledge my evolutionary roots, millennia deep, as a predatory omnivore. To participate actively in the bedrock workings of nature. For the atavistic challenge of doing it well with an absolute minimum of technological assistance. To learn the lessons, about nature and myself, that only hunting can teach. To accept personal responsibility for at least some of the deaths that nourish my life. For the glimpse it offers into wildness we can hardly imagine. Because it provides the closest thing I've known to a spiritual experience.

I hunt because it enriches my life and because I can't help myself ... because I was born with a hunter's heart.

David Petersen (ed.), *A Hunter's Heart: Honest Essays on Blood Sport*

The subject of ethics seems to stir up many hunters, mainly I think, because people feel somebody will judge their own ethics or try to inflict their opinions on others. After all, most think that ethics are a very personal thing, while others suspect that those who lay claim to any ethics whatsoever are hypocrites and their ethics count for nought when that hunter is away from home — in the back-country, where no one else is watching! However, even in the back-country there are natural laws governing the relationships between species and the environment, and we do well to not stand aloof from them but rather we should mesh into the natural order of things.

It certainly is a risky thing to set down in print in such a public forum my own code of ethics; but, hey, some people are so broad-minded they'll accept anything — and stand for nothing. I want to stand for something. We are free to make our own choices of course (and we take the consequences of those actions), but the judgments we do make depend somewhat on the mind we develop to make the choices in the first place!

I wanted to finish this book with a summary of *my* values around hunting and how my mind has been challenged or stretched. (I don't necessarily expect that you, the reader, will agree with all of my values or take all of these on board, but I do expect that you might assess your own standards. If this sample causes you to engage in some constructive discussion with other hunters, over a brew around the campfire, or to think and act with earnest intent on the hill, all well and good.)

I've noticed, too, that by seriously struggling with what I want to uphold and by introducing others to the values of my personal hunting code, I've actually strengthened those values in myself and increased my resolve to act with integrity.

Why close out this book on this note? I felt that without bringing ethics to the fore, it is more difficult to focus fully on what will help take our hunting heritage into the future. The magic of hunting memories such as those shared throughout this book must remain for generations to come and so I'm *compelled* to encourage others to be mindful of values, to strongly encourage you to think over what you hold precious in the *way* we hunt in New Zealand.

If hunting is to survive to be practised by those generations that come after me, then I must preserve, enhance and protect the mana and image of hunting and of hunters as guardians of the land and of our wild creatures. Having a transparent set of ethics may help demonstrate that point of view, with a sense of integrity and personal responsibility for upholding what we deem precious in our lifestyles.

As Theodore Roosevelt, hunter, conservationist and vigorous exemplar, said, 'We have duties to ourselves and duties to others — we cannot shirk either.'

Hunters, non-hunters and anti-hunters alike are calling for a creed — a set of beliefs or principles to hold to and which at their core demands respect for our wild places and the creatures that live there now. The ideas listed below have been developing in me over the years and I accept that my opinions have been adjusted over time — and quite probably will continue to do so.

My hunter's creed

- I will not be ashamed in society of my intention to kill an animal when I hunt. This clearly asserts that I intend to participate in the natural world that feeds me, rather than just merely observing it. 'Hunting to live' is an integral part of the way of things in the natural world and I want to be linked in to that process.

- I have full respect for the animals I hunt: respect for the quarry has been a consistent and fundamental theme in every hunting civilization. We are part of the same interdependent web of life and I will not demean wild creatures in word or actions with them.

- I will hunt 'fair chase': I want game animals to be free to use all their wild defences when I am hunting. Jim Posewitz's international organization for hunters, Orion, defines hunting as 'the fair chase pursuit of free-roaming wildlife in a non-competitive situation in which the animal is used for food'.

- I want more 'authentic' New Zealand-style hunts: I will be selective in the animals I kill and I will be selective in the way I hunt, so that I capture the essence of the hunt for me. As long as I'm able, I'd like to include elements of effort, adventure and challenge — where strenuous, hard hunts in wilderness country are preferred.

- I choose to minimize technological advantage: I will still hunt with a rifle and utilize modern outdoor living equipment, but I want to retain my intuition and learn more of the 'old knowledge', upholding certain more genuine aspects of traditional hunting. Therefore, I will continually develop my code to distinguish appropriate from inappropriate technology, discerning what sustains 'fair chase' rather than violating that concept for an inappropriate advantage over my quarry.

- I will kill for food: a kill will be a disciplined and mindful activity for me. Therefore I will use as much meat as possible. Even when taking an animal for a memento, or in culls for game management, I will still carry out and utilize the meat.
- I will increase and practise my skills: my mountaincraft, stalking, gunnery and marksmanship skills shall be such to effect a certain and quick kill at interactive ranges in the animal's own terrain. My goal is to fire all shots from at most within 300 metres.
- I will obey the regulations that apply to the areas I hunt. In other instances, where certain practices may be the norm, I will continue to challenge these methods as to whether they fit my creed. If the hunting situation can be manipulated to lure the animal, significantly reduce the animal's chance to survive or can override the instincts of animals in their wild territory, I will not engage in that type of hunt. (Heli-hunting is an example of an improper advantage that I consider unethical hunting.)
- I will minimize any trace of my having been in the mountains: this includes packing out my rubbish and that of others.
- I will get involved to help defend and secure the future of hunting and our wildlife. I can't separate my love of hunting and the outdoors from a passion for the environment and the truer participation of this way of living. Therefore I aim

to impact upon decision makers, other users of the outdoors and the general public. I also want to try to influence my companions accordingly as well as the media that is messaging this generation of hunters.

• I will ensure that hunting effort and the times spent in these wild, open places are together kept in their proper place and context — remembering my primary purpose is to know and love the Creator.

The next plateau in this saga is nurturing a hunting ethic capable of sustaining hunting in a society growing distant from nature, natural rhythms and the beauty of an honest association with wildness.

— Jim Posewitz